INHABITANTS

of

NEW HAMPSHIRE

1776

Emily S. Wilson

CLEARFIELD

Reprinted 1993 by arrangement
Genealogical Publishing Co., Inc.
Baltimore Maryland

Library of Congress Catalog Card Number 93-78018

Reprinted for Clearfield Company by
Genealogical Publishing Company
Baltimore, Maryland 2014

ISBN 978-0-8063-1384-9

INTRODUCTION

In March 1776 the Continental Congress resolved that all persons who refused to sign the Association to defend the cause of the colonies should be disarmed. To put this resolve into effect, the New Hampshire Committee of Safety directed the local authorities, usually the selectmen, to have all adult males sign the Association and to report the names of those who refused to sign.

The end result amounted to a census of the adult male inhabitants of New Hampshire for 1776, an invaluable genealogical reference source. There are some limits to the record. The returns for a few towns are missing while that for Exeter is fragmentary. In addition, some towns did not include the names of men who were away on service in the Continental Army. (A list of the towns included in the returns will be found on page 123.)

This record was originally published in Peter Force's *American Archives,* Series IV, volume 5 (1848), and subsequently in *Miscellaneous Revolutionary Documents of New Hampshire* edited by Albert S. Batchellor and published in 1910 as volume 30 of the New Hampshire State Papers Series. Both these publications, however, were arranged by town with the men's names listed in the order they signed. The present publication has placed these names, well over nine thousand, in one alphabetical sequence to enable a researcher to determine at a glance where representatives of a particular surname resided.

Some abbreviations have been used which are indicated below. In addition, a number in parenthesis indicates the number of men in a town having the same name.

n. Non-Associator, that is, a man who refused to sign the Association. Since these names were written by someone other than the man himself, they sometimes appear in the record in a very mutilated form.

Q. Quaker. Some towns made provision in their lists to name those who could not sign the Association because of religious scruples against bearing arms. However, it should be kept in mind that not all towns made this distinction.

s. Selectman. A few men signed the returns only in their official capacity as selectmen but did not actually sign the Association. This was probably an oversight in most instances.

The resolve of the Continental Congress and the order in its behalf by the New Hampshire Committee of Safety are printed in full below.

ASSOCIATION TEST
COLONY OF NEW HAMPSHIRE
IN COMMITTEE OF SAFETY
April 12th, 1776

In Order to carry the underwritten RESOLVE of the Hon'ble Continental CONGRESS into Execution, You are requested to desire all Males above Twenty One Years of Age (Lunaticks, Idiots, and Negroes excepted) to sign to the DECLARATION on this Paper; and when so done, to make Return hereof, together with the Name or Names of all who shall refuse to sign the same, to the GENERAL ASSEMBLY, or Committee of Safety of this Colony.

M. Weare, Chairman

In CONGRESS, March 14th, 1776

Resolved, That it be recommended to the several Assemblies, Conventions, and Councils, or Committees of Safety of the United Colonies, *immediately* to cause all Persons to be *disarmed,* within their Respective Colonies, who are *notoriously* disaffected to the Cause of AMERICA, Or who have not associated, and refuse to associate, to defend by ARMS, the United Colonies, against the Hostile Attempts of the British Fleets and Armies.

(COPY)   *Extract from the Minutes.*

Charles Thompson, Sec'ry.

In Consequence of the above Resolution, of the Hon. Continental CONGRESS, and to shew our Determination in joining our American Brethren, in defending the Lives, Liberties, and Properties of the Inhabitants of the UNITED COLONIES.

WE, the *Subscribers,* do hereby solemnly engage, and promise, that we will, to the utmost of our Power, at the Risque of our Lives and Fortunes, with ARMS, oppose the Hostile Proceedings of the British Fleets, and Armies, against the *United American* COLONIES.

Abbot, Abiel	Wilton		Adams - Cont'd	
Amos	Portsmouth		Israel	Rindge
Amos Jr.	Concord		Israel Jr.	Rindge
Daniel	Concord		Jacob, s.	Wilton
Darius	Amherst		James	Londonderry (2)
David	Pembroke		James Jr.	Londonderry
Ephraim	Concord		John	Packersfield
George	Concord		Jonathan	Gilsum
George Jr.	Concord		Jonathan	Londonderry
Isaac	Concord		Joseph	Dublin
Jabez	Concord		Joseph	Newington
Jacob	Wilton		Joseph	Stratham
Jeremiah	Wilton		Joseph Jr.	Stratham
Jesse	Concord		Josiah	Newmarket
Job	Pembroke		Moses	Dublin
John	Brentwood		Robert	Londonderry
Joseph	Concord		Samuel	Rindge
Joseph	Wilton		Timothy	Dublin
Joseph Jr.	Wilton		William	Monadnock
Nathan	Concord		William	Portsmouth
Reuben Jr.	Concord		Adkins, David	Claremont
Samuel	Pembroke		John	Claremont
Sam'l Jr.	Pembroke		Timothy	Claremont
Stephen	Concord		Agaton, Samuel	Boscawen
William	Wilton		Aiken, James	Chester
William Jr.	Wilton		James	Society Land
Abbott, Amos	Concord		John	Bedford
Edward	Concord		John	Londonderry
Ephraim	Amherst		Nenian	Deering
Ephraim	Deering		Thomas	Deering
Nath'l	Concord		William	Deering
Reuben	Concord		Aikin, James	Bedford
Wm.	Portsmouth		Aires, Wil'm	Chesterfield
Abell, Benjamin	Lempster		Airmet,	
Frederick	Lempster		Thomas, n.	Portsmouth
Phinehas	Lempster		Akarman,	
Abott, Benjamin	Concord		Barnet	Portsmouth
Adams,			Nahum	Portsmouth
Aaron (Capt) n., Henniker			Simeon	Portsmouth
Benj. Esq., n., Henniker			Walter	Portsmouth
Daniel	Rindge		Aken, Phinehas	Raby
David	Rindge		Akin, Peter	Chester
Ezekiel Gil	Newington		Samuel	Chester
Isaac	Dublin		Akerman, Benj.	Portsmouth

Akerman - Cont'd		Allen - Cont'd	
John	Portsmouth	Josiah	Allenstown
Joseph	Portsmouth	Josiah	Stratham
Albee, Abner	Chesterfield	Jude Jr.	Stratham
Alcock, Robert	Weare	Moses	Richmond
Alden, Adam	Claremont	Ruben	Gilmanton
James	Claremont	Samuel	Wakefield
Thomas	Dublin	Samuel Jr.	Wakefield
Aldrich,		William	Rochester
Aaron	Richmond	Alley, Sam'l	Rochester
Abner	Richmond	Alliene,	
Abner Jr.	Richmond	Elezer, n.	Deerfield
Ananias	Richmond	Allis, Abraham	Barrington
Artemis	Richmond	Allison, Sam'l	Dunbarton
Benj.	Westmoreland	Sam'l	Londonderry
Caleb	Westmoreland	Alls, Samuel	Londonderry
Nathan	Richmond	Amazeen,	
Peter	Richmond	Christopher	Newcastle
Solomon	Richmond	Ephraim	Newcastle
William	Richmond	John	Newcastle
Zibe	Richmond	Ambros, Robert	Concord
Alexander, Alaxander,		Ambrose, Nath'l	Pembroke
Asa	Winchester	Ame, Joel	Rye
Ebn'r	Winchester	Ames, David	Canterbury
James	Dunbarton	David	Peterborough
James	Londonderry (2)	Jacob, n.	Newmarket
John	Londonderry	John	Newmarket
John	Winchester	Nat	Newmarket
Jonas	Henniker	Nat Jr.	Newmarket
Reubin	Winchester	Samuel	Boscawen
Samuel	Bow	Samiel	Canterbury
Seth	Winchester	Samuel	Epsom
William	Londonderry (2)	Samuel Jr.	Epsom
Alkin, John	Winchester	Simon	Canterbury
Allaman, John	Hampton	Amsbry, Israel	Westmoreland
Allard, Henry	Rochester	Amy, Abraham	Salem
Allcock, Jos.	Portsmouth	Anderson, Ondrson,	
Allen,		David	Londonderry
Abel	Surry	James	Londonderry (3)
Abner	Wakefield	John	Londonderry
Ezra	Richmond	John	Windham
James, n.	Rochester	Robert	Londonderry
John (Capt) n.	Salem	Samuel	Londonderry (2)
Joseph	Richmond	Thomas	Candia

Anderson - Cont'd	
Thomaes	Londonderry
William	Londonderry
Andrews, Isaac	Hillsborough
Angier, Silas	Temple
Anis, Jesse	Londonderry
Annes, John	Londonderry
Ansden, Uriah	Henniker
Answorth,	
Edward	Claremont
Appleton, Wm.	Portsmouth
Archer, Benj.	Keene
Benj. Jr.	Keene
Jonathan	Keene
Archibald,	
Arthur	Londonderry
John	Londonderry
Robt.	Londonderry
Aris, see Ayers.	
Arlen, John	Barrington
Thomas	Lee
Armet, see Airmet.	
Armor, Andrew	Windham
Armour, Gain	Windham
Armstrong,	
David	Windham
John	Windham
John Jr.	Windham
Arnold, James	Portsmouth
Artherton, Aretherton,	
Jonathan	Richmond
Solomon	Richmond
Ashby, John, n.	Salem
Ashley, Daniel	Winchester
Oliver	Claremont
Sam'l	Claremont
Sam'l	Winchester
Aspenwall, Zalmon	Lebanon
Asten, John	Salem
Nathan, n.	Salem
Timothy	Temple
Astin, Abiel	Salem
Atherton,	
Joshua Esq., n.	Amherst

Atkenson,	
Benj.	Sandwich
Atkinson,	
Jonathan	Boscawen
Joseph	Boscawen
Nathaniel	Boscawen
Sam'l	Boscawen
Simeon	Boscawen
Theodore, n.	Portsmouth
Atwell,	
Richard, n.	Monadnock
Atwood,	
Caleb	Weare
David	Atkinson
James	Hampstead
John	Atkinson
John	Hampstead
John Jr.	Hampstead
Jonathan	Weare
Austin,	
Benj. Jr.	Portsmouth
Jon'a L.	Portsmouth
Moses, Q.	Rochester
Averall,	
Thomas Jr.	Amherst
Averial, John	Amherst
Averil,	
Ebenezer	Amherst
Avery; see also Havery;	
David	Gilmanton
John	Deerfield
John	Stratham
Jonathan	Temple
Joseph, n.	Gilmanton
Joshua	Stratham
Josiah	Gilmanton
Samuel	Gilmanton (2)
Axtell, John	Alstead
Ayer,	
John	Pembroke
Samuel	Salem
Samuel	Weare
Stephen	Dunbarton
William	Salem

Ayers, Aris; see also Eayers	
Edward	Portsmouth
Geo.	Portsmouth
Jonathan	Portsmouth
Joseph	Portsmouth
Perkins	Portsmouth
Sam'l	Portsmouth
Thomas	Portsmouth
Thoms.	Portsmouth
Ayes, John	Portsmouth
Babb, Benjamin	Barrington
John	Barrington
Richard	Barrington
Thomas	Epsom
William	Barrington
Bachelder; see also Batchelder.	
Abraham	Loudon
Daniel	Loudon
Daves	Northwood
Elisha	Hawke
Francses	Deerfield
Jathro Jr.	Loudon
Jethro	Loudon
Jeremiah	Kensington
John Jr.	Deerfield
John	Kensington
Jonathan	Gilmanton
Josiah	East Kingston
Lebe	Loudon
Nathan	Loudon
Nathanael 3d	Deerfield
Phinehas	Sandown
Stephen Jr.	Deerfield
Bacheller, Bachellor, Bachelor; see also Batcheler.	
Ebenezer	East Kingston
Nathan	East Kingston
Nath'l	East Kingston
Nathaniel	Loudon
Nath'l Gilman	East Kingston
Phinas	East Kingston
Simon	East Kingston
Thomas	East Kingston
Bacor, see Baker.	

Badger, Ezra	Concord
James	Raby
Joseph	Gilmanton
Joseph Jr.	Gilmanton
Nath'l	Raby
Peaslee	Gilmanton
Stephen	Kingston
William, n.	Newmarket
Baglay,	
Jonathan	Candia
Bagly, Jacob	Candia
Bailash, Philip	Packersfield
Bailey,	
Ebenezer	Westmoreland
Jesse	Newport
Joel	Newport
John	Londonderry
Luther	Westmoreland
Sam'l	Lebanon
Sam'l Jr.	Lebanon
Solomon	Piermont
Bain, Joseph	Newmarket
Baker, Bacor,	
Benj.	Derryfield
Benjamin, n.	Hinsdale
Epharim	Wilton
Jesse	Derryfield
Joseph	Bow
Joseph	Pembroke
Lovewell	Pembroke
Moses	Candia
Samuel	Newmarket
Thos.	Keene
Thos. Jr.	Keene
Thomas	Pembroke
William	Candia
Balch, Andrew	Keene
Benj.	Keene
John	Keene
Nath'el	Wakefield
Nathanael Jr.	Wakefield
Baldwin Daniel	Chesterfield
Ephraim	Chesterfield
John	Lebanon

Baldwin - Cont'd	
Nahum	Amherst
Rufus	Lebanon
Thos	Canaan
Bale, see Bayl.	
Bales, see Baols, Bayl.	
Baley, see also Bayley.	
Jonathan	Salem
Joshua	Salem
William	Atkinson
Ball, Nath'l	Temple
Peter	Portsmouth
Jonathan	Rindge
Samuel	Portsmouth
Samuel Jr.	Portsmouth
Ballard, N.	Wilton
Uriah	Wilton
Ballord, Jeremiah	Hampton
Ballou, Below,	
Jeams	Richmond
Matturean	Richmond
Seth	Richmond
Silas	Richmond
Bamford, see also Bumford.	
Robart	Barrington
Bancroft, Benj.	Rindge
Caleb	Temple
James	Packersfield
Banfil, Charls.	Portsmouth
John, n.	Nottingham
John	Portsmouth
Joseph	Portsmouth
Tobias	Portsmouth
Baols, Jonathan	Richmond
Barber, Daniel	Epping
Robart	Newmarket
Robart Jr.	Newmarket
Robard	Salisbury
Zeblon	Newmarket
Bard, William	Pembroke
Barit, see Barrit.	
Barker,	
Benjamin	Stratham
Daniel	Wilton

Barker - Cont'd	
Ebenezer, n.,	Stratham
Eph'm	Amherst
Ezra	Stratham
John, n.	Epping
Jonathan, n.	Epping
Nathan, n.	Stratham
Nathaniel, n.	Hopkinton
Noah	Nottingham
Philbrok	Lee
William, n.	Monadnock
Barnard, Benj.	South Hampton
Jacob	South Hampton
Joseph	Hopkinton
Moses	Deerfield
Stephen	Hawke
Barnet, John	Londonderry
John Jr.	Londonderry
Barnett, James	Londonderry
Mos.	Londonderry
Barney, Barnay,	
Constant	Richmond
David	Richmond
Barns, Asa	Bedford
Bill	Claremont
Jon'a	Hillsborough
Darran, William	Surry
Barret,	
Aaron, n.	Hinsdale
Isaac	Nottingham West
James	Londonderry
John	Hinsdale
Moses	Hinsdale
Moses	Londonderry
Moses	Nottingham West
Nathaniel	Amherst
Simeon	Nottingham West
Barrit, Barit,	
Isaacs	Hinsdale
Jonathan	Hinsdale
Silas	Hinsdale
Zadock	Hinsdale
Barron,	
Moses	Amherst

[9]

Barrus,	
Abraham	Richmond
Abraham Jr.	Richmond
Ebenezer	Richmond
John	Richmond
Michael	Richmond
Oliver	Richmond
Barry, Simon	Chester
Bartlet, Abiel	Deerfield
Eben'r	Kingston
Gideon	Canterbury
John, n.,	Deerfield
John, n.,	Deering
John	Kingston
John, n.,	Nottingham
Jonathan	Pembroke
Joshua	Kingston
Josiah	Lee
Matthias	East Kingston
Nathan Jr.	Kingston
Philip, n.,	Nottingham
Richard	Pembroke
Samuel	Northwood
Stephen	Pembroke
Thomas	Nottingham
Timothy	Kingston
Bartlett,	
George	Hawke
Jacob	Londonderry
John	Epping
John	Newmarket
John	Portsmouth
Joseph	Salisbury
Joshua Jr.	Kingston
Josiah	Kingston
Josiah Hall	Newmarket
Barton, Stephen	Newcastle
Basford,	
Ebenezer	Chester
Jon'n, n.,	Henniker
Joseph	Salisbury
Bass,	
Joseph	Portsmouth
Bassit, Sam'l	Keene

Batchelder; see also Bachelder.	
Abraham	Northwood
Benj.	Candia
Benjamin	Deerfield
Benjamin	Hampton
Carter	Hampton
Daniel	Wilton
David	Deerfield
Ephraim	Deerfield
Hanery	North Hampton
Henry	North Hampton
Increas	Northwood
Isaac	Gilmanton
James	North Hampton
John	Deerfield
John	Hampton
John	Northwood
Joseph	Kensington
Josiah	Hawke
Josiah	Kensington
Josiah	North Hampton
Nathaniel	Hampton
Nathaniel	North Hampton
Samuel	North Hampton
Simon	Deerfield
Stephen	Deerfield
Stephen 3d	Deerfield
Zaceriah	North Hampton
Batcheldor,	
Samuel	North Hampton
Batcheler, Batchelor; see also	
Bacheller.	
Increase	Deerfield
Nathan	Deerfield
Batchellor,	
Breed (Major) n.,	Packersfield
Bate, Nath'l	Dublin
Bates, David	Claremont
Batson, Nath'l	Newcastle
Stephen, n.,	Newcastle
Battey, Silvanus	Chesterfield
Baxter,	
Simon, n.	Alstead
Simon Jr.	Alstead

Baxter - Cont'd	
Thomas	Canaan
Baybrick,	
Theophelus	Lebanon
Bayl, Bayls; see also Baols.	
John	Deering
William	Wilton
William Jr.	Wilton
Bayley, see also Baley.	
Abner	Salem
Daniel	Weare
David	Salem
Dudley	Atkinson
Ebenezer	Weare
James	Atkinson
Jesse	Weare
John	Salem
John Jr.	Salem
John Moor	Salem
Jonathan Jr.	Salem
Joseph	Sandown
Joshua	Hampton
Joshua Jr.	Salem
Moses	Hopkinton
Samuel, n.,	Weare
Simon	Chester
William	Salem
Bayls, see Bayl, Baols.	
Beacham, Rich'd	Sanbornton
Beal, see also Beel.	
Josiah	Exeter
William	Packersfield
Beals, see Baols.	
Bean, see also Been.	
Benjamin	Bow
Benj.	Salisbury
Benj.	Sandwich
David	Candia
David	Gilmanton
David	Sandwich
Georg	Meredith
Gideon	Gilmanton
James, n.	Nottingham
Jeremiah	Kingston

Bean - Cont'd	
John	Canterbury
John	Newmarket
Joseph	Boscawen
Joseph	East Kingston
Joseph Esq., n.	Salisbury
Joshua, n.,	Gilmanton
Josiah	Sandwich
Jude	Gilmanton
Phinehas	Salisbury
Samuel	Sandown
Simeon	Gilmanton
Sinkler, n.,	Salisbury
Stephen	Gilmanton
Beard, William	New Boston
Beck, Andrew	Portsmouth
Henry	Concord
John	Portsmouth
John Jr.	Portsmouth
Sam'll	Portsmouth
Samuel	Portsmouth
William	Portsmouth
Beckwith, Abel	Alstead
Andrew	Alstead
Jabez	Lempster
Bedel, Thomas	Boscawen
Beede,	
Aaron, n.,	Sandwich
Daniel	Sandwich
Daniel Jr.	Sandwich
Nathan, n.,	Sandwich
Beedy, Hezekiah	Kingston
Beel, see also Beal.	
Aaron	Packersfield
Been, see also Bean.	
James, n.,	Brentwood
Jeremiah, n.	Brentwood
John	Salisbury
Joshua, n.	Brentwood
Levi, n.,	Brentwood
Richard, n.	Brentwood
Richard Jr., n.	Brentwood
William, n.	Brentwood
William	Sandown

Belagh, William	Stratham
Belding, Moses	Winchester
Stephen	Winchester
Belknap, Moses	Atkinson
Nath'l	Salem
Belknop, Ezekiel	Atkinson
Bell, Abednego	Newcastle
Benj. Jr.	Newcastle
John	Bedford
John	Londonderry
Joseph	Bedford
Joseph	Londonderry
Matthew	Newcastle
Meshack Jr.	Newcastle
Meshach 3d	Newcastle
Sampson	Newcastle
Thomas	Newcastle
Below, see Ballou.	
Bemies, Biemies,	
Henry	Packersfield
Timothy	Monadnock
Ben, Benjamin	Deerfield
Bennet, Cotton	Newmarket
David	Sandown
John	Brentwood
John Jr.	Brentwood
John	Newmarket
Josiah	Newmarket
Moses	Westmoreland
Silas, n.,	Chesterfield
Spencer	Sandown
Bennett, Arthur	Newmarket
Ephraim	Portsmouth
John Jr.	Newmarket
Thomas	Newmarket
Benson, Isaac	Richmond
John	Newington
Joseph	Portsmouth
Beray, Epheraim	Epsom
Berey, Jacob	Rye
Bergin, Beargin; see also Burgen.	
John	Rochester
Berrey, Stephen	Rochester
Berry, Ealet	Chester

Berry – Cont'd	
George	Barrington
Jeremiah	Rye
Jeremiah Jr.	Rye
Joatham	Rye
John	Barrington
Jonthan	Chester
Merifeld	Rye
Nat	Barrington
Samuel	Barrington
Stephen	Barrington
William Jr.	Rye
Bettes, Jonathan	Lebanon
Bettison, Naboth	Keene
Betton, James	Windham
Bevens, John	Saville
Bickford,	
Benj., n.,	Rochester
Daniel	Barnstead
Dep.	Newington
Henry	Portsmouth
Ichabod	Newington
John	Barnstead
John	Nottingham
John	Northwood
Jon'a	Rochester
Lemuel	Rochester
Micajah	Lee
Paul	Gilmanton
Samuel	Lee
Solomon	Northwood
Thomas	Hopkinton
Thomas	Nottingham
Tho.	Portsmouth
Bicknell,	
Nathan	Enfield
Bigelow, Benj.	Portsmouth
Bill, David	Gilsum
Ebenezer	Gilsum
Bingham,	
Elijah	Lempster
Elisha	Enfield
Jonathan	Lebanon
Nath'l	Chesterfield

Bingham - Cont'd

Reuben	Lempster
Silas	Lempster
Theodorus	Chesterfield
Bishop, John	Chesterfield
Nathan	Chesterfield
Samuel	Monadnock
Bixbe, Andrew	Hillsborough
Bixby, Benj.	Salem
Benjamin Jr.	Salem
Blacke, Paul	Kensington
Philemon	Kensington
Blair, John, n.	New Boston
John	Peterborough
William	New Boston

Blaisdell, see also Blasdall, Blasdel.

John	Hopkinton
Blak, Darbon	Epping

Blake, Blaake,

Asahel	Keene
Asahel	Northwood
Ebenezer	Epping
Elijah	Keene
Elisha	Barrington
Elisha	Kensington
Elisha Jr.	Kensington
Hesekiah	Kensington
Hezekiah	Hawke
Jedidiah	Epping
Jesse	Weare
Jethery	Hampton
Jethro	Epsom
John	Barrington
John	Weare
Jonathan	Atkinson
Jonathan	Hampton
Jonathan	Hawke
Jonathan Jr.	Hawke
Jonathan	Northwood
Joseph	Epping
Joseph	Keene
Moses	Kensington
Nathan	Hampton

Blake - Cont'd

Nathan	Keene
Nathan Jr.	Keene
Nicolas	Northwood
Obadiah Jr.	Keene
Oliver Smith	Sandown
Pain	Epping
Philemon Jr.	Kensington
Phinehas	Northwood
Robert, n.	Epping
Royal	Keene
Samuel	Epsom
Samuel	Hampton
Sherbun	Northwood
Theophilus	Epping
William	Northwood

Blanchard, Blachard,

Amos	Concord
Benjamin	Canterbury
Benj. 3d	Canterbury
Benj.	Sandwich
Benj.	Wilton
Daniel	Westmoreland
David	Wilton
Edward	Canterbury
Georg.	Wilton
James	Canterbury
Jonathan	Canterbury
Joseph	Chester
Joshua	Wilton
Joth.	Peterborough
Richard	Canterbury
Stephen	Wilton

Blancher, David   Canterbury

Blanshard,

Benjamin Jr.	Canterbury

Blasdall, see also Blaisdell.

Nathanal	Chester

Blasdel, Abner   Portsmouth

Daniel	East Kingston
Henry	East Kingston
Isaac	Chester
Jacob	East Kingston
Jacob	Epping

Blasdel - Cont'd		Bohonon - Cont'd	
John	East Kingston	Jecob	Salisbury
Jonathan	East Kingston	Boid, see Boyd.	
Jonathan	Weare	Boienton, see Boynton.	
Moses	East Kingston	Boies, see also Boyes, Boys.	
Olliver	Loudon	John	Bedford
Ralph	East Kingston	Thomas	Bedford
Ralph	Kingston	Bois, Samuel	Londonderry
Samuel	Amherst	Bond, Henry	Winchester
Thomas	Deerfield	Isaac	Dublin
Blasdell, Wm.	Wakefield	John	Exeter
Bliss, Abner	Gilsum	John	Hampstead
Azariah	Lebanon	John Jr.	Hampstead
Azariah Jr.	Lebanon	Samuel	Winchester
Daniel	Lebanon	Stephen	Gilsum
David	Gilsum	Stephen Jr.	Gilsum
Ebenezer	Lebanon	Boodey, John	Barrington
Isaiah	Lebanon	Boorn, Amos	Richmond
Jonathan	Gilsum	Booth,	
Jonathan Jr.	Gilsum	Freegrace	Lempster
Levi	Gilsum	George	Hillsborough
Stephen	Lebanon	Oliver	Lempster
Blodget, Bloget,		Boutell, Joseph	Amherst
Asahel	Nottingham West	Bouttel, Reuben	Amherst
Jermiah	Nottingham West	Bouttle, Joseph	Amherst
Jonathen	Nottingham West	Boutwell, Kendall	Amherst
Joseph	Nottingham West	Bowden, Michael	Saville
Blodgett, Jacob	Amherst	Bowen, Bowin, Boen,	
Blood, Ebenezer	Deering	John	Salisbury
Francis	Temple	Thomas	Richmond
Blue, Edward	Deerfield	Bowers,	
Jonathan	Deerfield	Nehemiah	Rindge
Blunt, Ephraim	Loudon	Bowles, John	Boscawen
Epheaim Jr.	Loudon	John Jr.	Boscawen
John	Rye	Sam'l	Portsmouth
Samuel	Chester	Thos.	Portsmouth
Wm.	Portsmouth	Bowman, And'w	Newmarket
Bly, William	Lee	Jonas	Henniker
Bodge, Benjamin	Lee	Boyce, Paul	Richmond
Samuel (Mr.)	Lee	Boyd, Boyed, Boid,	
Boen, see Bowen.		Alex'dr	Londonderry
Bohonan, Annieas	Salisbury	Arthur	Londonderry
Bohonon, Andrew	Salisbury	J'o.	Portsmouth
Andrew Jr.	Salisbury	Joseph	Society Land

Boyd - Cont'd
Nathaniel	Derryfield
Robert	Londonderry
Robert Jr.	Londonderry
Robart, n.,	New Boston
Samuel	Derryfield
Samuel	New Boston
Thomas	Londonderry
William	Londonderry

Boyes, see also Boies, Bois.
James	Londonderry
Robert	Londonderry
William (Lieut.)	New Boston
Boys, Joseph	Londonderry
Boynton, John	Gilsum
John Jr.	Gilsum
Joseph	Westmoreland
Joshua	Canterbury
Samuel	Stratham
William	Loudon
Bozard, Jonathan	Richmond

Brackenbury,
Samuel	Hopkinton

Bracket,
Ebenezer	Epsom
Brackett, Bening	Newmarket
Ich'd	Newmarket
James	Lee
Joseph	Lee
Joshua	Newmarket
Joshua	Portsmouth

Bradbury,
Ephraim	Saville
John	Loudon
Sanders	Nottingham West

Bradford,
Andrew	Amherst
Benj.	Deering
Enos	Amherst
John	Amherst
John	Salem
Samuel	Hillsborough
Simon	Salem
Timothy	Hillsborough

Bradford - Cont'd
William	Amherst
William	Deering

Bradley, Bradlay,
Jeremiah	Concord
John	Concord
Jonathan	Nottingham West
Josiah	Chester
Timothy	Concord
Timothy Jr.	Concord

Bradshaw,
Joshua	Hampstead
Brady, Benjamin	Lee
Bragg, Luther	Keene
Bragge, Benjamin	Newport
Brainerd, Asaph	Lempster
Shubael	Lempster
Uriah	Lempster

Branscombe,
Will'm	Hampton
Brasa, Samuel	Nottingham

Brassbridge,
Edward	Newington

Breed,
Eben'r, Q	Weare
Nath'l	Packersfield
Nathanael Jr.	Packersfield
Zep'h, Q	Weare

Breney, see McBreney.
Brett, Seth	Winchester
Seth Jr.	Winchester
Brewer, Isaac	Temple
Jas.	Monadnock

Brewstar,
Samuel	Barrington

Brewster,
Caleb	Portsmouth
Daniel	Portsmouth
David	Londonderry
David	Portsmouth
Isaac	Londonderry
John	Rochester
Moses	Portsmouth
Paul	Barrington

Brewster - Cont'd

William	Portsmouth
Briard, Jn'o.	Portsmouth
Samuel	Portsmouth
Brickett, Barnard	Chester
Brien, John	Bedford
Briggs, Caleb	Westmoreland
Eliphalet	Keene
Eliphalet Jr.	Keene
Elisha	Keene
Nath'l	Keene
Brigham, Abner	Croydon
Ephraim	Alstead
Britton, David	Westmoreland
William	Westmoreland
Brittun,	
Ebenezer	Westmoreland
Ebenezer 2d	Westmoreland
Seth	Westmoreland
Brock, Nicholas	Barrington
Brockelbank,	
Samuel	Weare
Brockway,	
William	Westmoreland
Woolston	Surry
Brook,	
Cornelius, n.	Claremont
Brooks,	
Abraham	Monadnock
Barnabas, n.	Claremont
Benjamin,	
(Capt.) n.	Claremont
Benjamin Jr., n.	Claremont
Samuel	Gilmanton
Simon	Alstead
Broten, John	Portsmouth
Brotten, Benj.	Portsmouth
Joseph	Portsmouth
Brown,	
Aaron	Candia
Aaron	Peterborough
Aaron, n.	Westmoreland
Abel	South Hampton
Abijah	Packersfield

Brown - Cont'd

Abra'm	Alstead
Abraham Jr.	Alstead
Abraham, n.	East Kingston
Abraham	Epping
Abraham Jr.	Epping
Abraham, n.	Hopkinton
Benjamin	Barnstead
Benjamin	Epping
Benjamin Jr.	Epping
Benj., n.	Hopkinton
Benj.	Kensington
Benjamin	North Hampton
Benjamin	South Hampton
Caleb, n.	Kensington
Clark, s.	Raby
David	Kensington
David	Newport
Ebenezer Jr.	Deerfield
Ebenezer	Wilton
Elias	Alstead
Eliphelit	Sanbornton
Elisha	Seabrook
Ephraim, n.	Deerfield
Ephraim	Temple
Ephraim	Westmoreland
Ezekiel	Epping
Francis	Brentwood
Hugh	Windham
Isaac	Seabrook
Isaac	South Hampton
Jacob	Newmarket
Jacob	North Hampton
James	Deerfield
Job	Rye
John Jr.	Barrington
John	Bow
John	North Hampton
John	Nottingham
John	Seabrook
John	Temple
John	Wilton
Jonathan	Candia
Jon'a	Kensington

Brown - Cont'd		Brown - Cont'd	
Jonathan	Rye	Timothy	Hawke
Joseph	Alstead	Timothy	Seabrook
Joseph	Barrington	William	Chester (2)
Joseph	Hampstead	William	Kensington
Joseph	Hawke	William	Wilton
Joseph	Kensington	Zecheriah	Hampton
Joseph Jr.	Kensington	Bryant,	
Joshua	Epping	Andrew	Hampstead
Joshua Jr.	North Hampton	Joseph	Barnstead
Josiah	Kensington	Richard	Pembroke
Josiah	Weare	Robert	Meredith
Josier	Barrington	Bryent, Jeremy	Newmarket
Moses	Hampstead	John	Bow
Moses	Hampton	Walter	Newmarket
Moses	Rochester	Walter Jr.	Newmarket
Moses	Westmoreland	Bryer, John	Sanbornton
Nathan	Hampton	Buel, Aaron	Newport
Nathaniel	Hawke	Daniel	Newport
Nathaniel	Londonderry	Joseph	Newport
Nehemiah	Candia	Buell, Abraham	Newport
Nichles	Barrington	Buffum, Jedidiah	Richmond
Nicholes	Nottingham	Bullard, Simeon	Dublin
Peter	Temple	Bullock,	
Philip	East Kingston	Jeremiah	Richmond
Phinehas	Chesterfield	Nathan	Richmond
Reuben	Deerfield	Bumford, see also Bamford.	
Rich	Unity	Charles	Barrington
Richard, s.	Rye	Jacob	Sanbornton
Robert	Leavitt's Town	Bump, see Mump.	
Samuel	Candia	Bunker, Buncker,	
Samuel	Chester	Dodefor	Barnstead
Sam'l	Hampstead	James, n.	Lee
Sam'l Jr.	Hampstead	Jonathan	Barnstead
Sam'l	Hampton	Joseph	Barnstead
Samuel Jr.	Hampton	Bunten, Andrew	Allenstown
Samuel	Hinsdale	John	Allenstown
Samuel	Sandwich	Burbank, Aaron	Epsom
Sewall	Candia	Abner	Brentwood
Simon	North Hampton	Caleb	Hopkinton
Stephen	Kensington	David	Boscawen
Stephen Jr.	Kensington	David	Brentwood
Thomas	Rochester	Ebenezer	Conway
Thomas Jr.	Rochester	John	Hopkinton

Burbank - Cont'd

Moses	Boscawen
Moses Jr.	Boscawen
Samuel	Boscawen
Samuel	Nottingham West
Samuel	Nottingham West
Samuel Jr.	Nottingham West
Burell, Thos	Amherst
Burgen,	
Ed Hall, n.,	Allenstown
Burleigh, Berly,	
John	Newmarket
Josiah	Lee
Samuel	Newmarket
Thomas	Sandwich
Burley, Jacob	Newmarket
John	Chester
John	Stratham
Josah	Newmarket
Moses	Newmarket
Nat'l	Sanbornton
Samuel	Lee
Stephen	Sanbornton
William	Newmarket
William Jr.	Newmarket
Burly, David	Stratham
Thomas	Epping
Wheeler	Stratham
Burman, Amos	Kingston
Burnam, Burnum,	
Abraham, n.	Dunbarton
Asa	Dunbarton
Ebeneser	Lee
Jacob	Nottingham
Joshua	Lee (2)
Nathan	Dunbarton
Offo	Hinsdale
Samuel	Dunbarton
Samuel	Nottingham
Stephen	Amherst
Burnap, Nathan	Dublin
Samuel	Temple
Burnham, Gideon	Westmoreland
Josiah	Newmarket

Burns, George	Amherst
George	Nottingham West
George Jr.	Nottingham West
John	Amherst (2)
John Jr.	Amherst
John	Bedford
John, n.	New Boston
Robert	Bedford
Robert	New Boston
Thomas	Amherst
William	Bedford
William	Nottingham West
Burnum, see Burnam.	
Buroughs, see Burroughs.	
Burpee, Jera'h	Candia
Nath'l	Candia
Burrell, see Burell.	
Burroughs, Buroughs, Buorroghs,	
Daniel	Alstead
George	Londonderry
Joel	Alstead
John	Alstead
John Jr.	Alstead
Josiah	Londonderry
Timothy	Alstead
William	Londonderry
Burt, Amasa	Winchester
Enos	Westmoreland
Joseph	Westmoreland
Burts, Robart	Canaan
Burton,	
Abraham	Wilton
John	Wilton (2)
Jno. Jr.	Wilton
Jon'a.	Wilton
Busel, Daniel	Kingston
James	Bow
Nathaniel	Sandown
William	Hawke
Buss, Silas	Wilton
Stephen	Wilton
Bussell; see also Busel.	
Nathaniel Jr.	Sandown
Buswell, Caleb	Concord

Buswell - Cont'd	
James, n.	Hopkinton
John	Rindge
Sam'l	Candia
Sam'l	Kingston
Butler, Buttler,	
Alford, n.	Portsmouth
Benjamin	Nottingham
Edm'd	Portsmouth
Henry	Nottingham
Jno.	Peterborough
John Jr.	Winchester
Josiah, n.	Hinsdale
Thos., n.	Hinsdale
Tobias	New Boston
Zephaniah	Nottingham
Butterfield,	
Abraham	Wilton
Eph'm (Capt) n.	Wilton
Isaac	Society Land
James	Westmoreland
John	Chester
John, n.	Westmoreland
Jonas	Westmoreland
Jos.	Wilton
Stephen	Wilton
Butters, Samuel	Concord
Buxton, James, Q	Weare
Buzzel, John, n.	Barrington
Samuel	Barrington
Thomas	Barrington
Buzzell, Benjamin	Barrington
Byam, Benj.	Temple
Cady[?], David	Winchester
Cairns, James	Bedford
Caldwell, Calldwell,	
Alexander	Nottingham West
James	Bedford
James	New Boston
James	Nottingham West
James Jr.	Nottingham West
James	Windham
Jno.	Nottingham West
Joseph	Nottingham West

Caldwell - Cont'd	
Samuel	Nottingham West
Sam'l	Weare
Thomas	Dunbarton
Thomas	Nottingham West
William	Bedford
Calef, John	Kingston
John Jr.	Kingston
William	Salisbury
Calf, Robt.	Chester
Calfe, John	Hampstead
Joseph	Kingston
William	Kingston
Call, David	Portsmouth
Moses	Boscawen (2)
Silas	Boscawen
Stephen	Salisbury
Calley; see also Cauley, Kalley	
Jonathan	Epping
Samuel	Stratham
Thomas Jr.	Epping
William	Stratham
William Jr.	Stratham
Cally, Eliphalet	Epping
Camball, see Campell.	
Cammet,	
Jonathan	Candia
Silas	Candia
Cammett, John	Candia
Campbel, David	Londonderry
Henry	Londonderry
Sam'l	Windham
Campbell,	
Alexander	Londonderry
Andrew	Salem
Henry	Windham
Hinry	Windham
Hugh	Bedford
Hugh	Salem
Hugh Jr.	Salem
James	Raby
James	Windham
John	Nottingham West
John, n.	Portsmouth

Campbell - Cont'd		**Carr - Cont'd**	
John	Windham	John	Brentwood
Robert	New Boston	John Jr.	Brentwood
William	New Boston	John	Candia
Campell, Camball,		John	Epping
Annes	Hawke	John 2nd	Epping
David	Henniker	John	Wakefield
Robard, n.	Henniker	Joseph	Canterbury
Cample, Daniel, n.	Amherst	Joseph	Chester
Capron, Oliver	Richmond	Mark	Chester
Card, Edward	Newcastle	Parker	Chester
Henry	Newcastle	Samuel	Meredith
John	Newcastle	Sanders	Kingston
Carew, see also Cario.		Timothy	Chester
Mich'l	Kingston	**Carswell; see also Caswel.**	
Carigain, Philip	Concord	Elijah	Northwood
Cario, Wm.	Newmarket	Richard	Northwood
Carleton, Jonathan	Hampstead	**Carter, Benj.**	Portsmouth
Carlton, Benj.	Rindge	Daniel	Concord
Dean	Acworth	David	Boscawen
Edward	Bow	Ephraim	Canterbury
James	Rindge	Ephraim	South. Hampton
John	Pembroke	Henry	Portsmouth
John	Salem	Jacob	Concord
Joseph	Salem	Jacob	Kingston
Kimball	Chesterfield	Jacob Jr.	Kingston
Oliver	Amherst	John	East Kingston
William	Pembroke	John	New Boston
William	Rindge	Moses	Kingston
Carpenter,		Samuel	East Kingston
Abisha	Winchester	Samuel Jr.	East Kingston
Benjamin	Surry	Thomas	Kingston
Eben'r	Keene	Winthrop	Boscawen
Eliph't	Keene	**Cartlin,**	
Jedidiah	Keene	Joseph, n.	Lee
Jonathan	Surry	**Cartty, John**	Exeter
Nathan	Surry	**Caruth, James**	Kingston
Samuel	Richmond	"born in Scotland"	
Carr; see also Karr.		**Cary, Barnabas**	Rindge
Bradbury	Chester	William	Lempster
David	Bow	**Case, Zenes**	Piermont
Ezekiel	Weare	**Casey, John**	Epsom
Francis	Chester	**Cass, Benja'n**	Candia
John	Bow	Daniel	Richmond

Cass - Cont'd			Chadbourn,	
Daniel Jr.	Richmond		Thomas	Conway
David	Richmond		Chadwick,	
John, n.	Epsom		Edmund	Boscawen
John	Richmond (2)		John	Hopkinton
Jonathan	East Kingston		Chale, see Chele.	
Jonathan	Sanbornton		Challes,	
Joseph	Richmond		Wellam	Kingston
Joseph Jr.	Richmond		Challis, John	Salisbury
Levi	Epsom		Chamberlain,	
Luke	Richmond		Abihail	Loudon
Simon	Epsom		Increas	Westmoreland
Caswel; see also Carswell.			Isaac	Westmoreland
Timothy	Northwood		James	Rochester
Cate, John	Barrington		Job, n.	Westmoreland
John	Epsom		Samuel	Loudon (2)
Joseph	Barrington		Samuel	Rochester
Sam'l	Deerfield		Simon	Winchester
Samuel	Portsmouth		Thomas	Westmoreland
Samuel White	Portsmouth		Wm	Rochester
Solomon	Barrington		Chamberlan,	
Stephen	Stratham		Ithamar	Chesterfield
William Jr.	Barrington		Chambers; see Chabers.	
Wm. Jr.	Portsmouth		Chamblen,	
Cater, Edward	Barrington		James	Dublin
Ezekiel	Concord		Chamberlin,	
Ezra	Concord		Henery	Westmoreland
John	Barrington		Jedidiah	Westmoreland
Levi	Pembroke		John	Westmoreland
Cates, Elisha	Sanbornton		Champney,	
James	Sanbornton		Rich'd	Portsmouth
James Jr.	Sanbornton		Chandler,	
Samuel	Loudon		Aaron	Westmoreland
Cats, Enoch	Sanbornton		Abner	Piermont
Cauley; see also Calley, Cally.			Benjamin	Portsmouth
John	Epping		Den'l	Concord
Thomas	Epping		Ebenezer	Wilton
Caveno, John, n.	Barrington		Isaac	Hopkinton
Caverly, John	Barrington		Joel	Alstead
Philip	Barrington		Jonathan	Piermont
Thomas, n.	Barrington		Joseph	Atkinson
Cavies, Nathaniel	Bow		Joseph	Epping (2)
Chabers,			Joseph	Hopkinton
Wm., n.	Henniker		Nathan	Concord

Chandler - Cont'd	
Nathaniel	Northwood
Samuel, n.	Alstead
Samuel	Deering
Zebulon	Alstead
Zechariah	Bedford
Chapin, Aaron	Surry
Hiram	Surry
Justus	Surry
Chaplin, Ebenezer	Rindge
Chapman, David	Newmarket
Edmund	Epping
Jeremiah	Rindge
John	Epping
John Jr.	Epping
John	Gilsum
Joseph	Londonderry
Joseph	Newmarket
Sam'l	Keene
Samuel	Newmarket
Samuel	North Hampton
Sam'l	Stratham
Simeon	Epsom
Chas, Jacob	Londonderry
Chase, Chaes,	
Abner	Unity
Abraham	Hawke
Amos	Unity
Charles	Seabrook
Danieal	Concord
Daniel	Seabrook
Dudley	Weare
Dudley L.	Stratham
Ebenezer	Brentwood
Edmund	Newmarket
Edward, n.	Stratham
Elihu, Q	Kensington
Elihu Jr., Q	Kensington
Enoch	East Kingston
Ezekiel	Nottingham West
James	Epping
James Jr.	Epping
John	Concord
John, Q	Kensington

Chase - Cont'd	
John	North Hampton
John, n.	Salem
John ,	Seabrook
John, n.	Weare
Jonathan	Epping
Jonathan	Hopkinton
Jonathan Jr.	Seabrook
Jon'a.	Sanbornton
Jonathan	Stratham
Jonathan Jr.	Stratham
Joshua	Nottingham West
Josiah	Deerfield
Josiah	Epping
Moody	Chester
Moses	Deerfield
Moses	Stratham
Nathan, Q	Kensington
Nathaniel	Brentwood
Nathanil	Hampstead
Nathaniel, Q	Kensington
Nathaniel	Winchester
Nehemiah	Seabrook
Seth	Croydon
Stephen	Deerfield
Stephen, Q	Kensington
Stephen Jr.	Newcastle
Stephen	Nottingham West
Stephen Jr.	Nottingham West
Thomas	Sandown
Wells	Chester
William	Stratham
Chattell, Thomas	Gilmanton
Chatterton,	
Joseph	Acworth
Chele, Daniel	Lee
Gerge	Lee
Chellis,	
Thones	Hawke
Cheney,	
Benjamin	Londonderry
Daniel	Londonderry
Isaac	Dunbarton
James	Londonderry

Cheney - Cont'd	
John	Society Land
Moses	Brentwood
Tristram	Society Land
Chesamor, Jacob	Dunbarton
Chesle, John	Nottingham
Sawyer	Nottingham

Chesley,
Ebenezer	Rochester
James	Rochester
Lemuel	Lee

Cheswill,
Wentworth	Newmarket
Child, Amos	Packersfield
Choate, Jacob	Hopkinton

Christy, see Cristy.

Church,
Ebenezer	Gilsum
James	Barrington
James	Newport
John	Barrington
John	Dunbarton
Nathaniel	Barrington
Churchill, Thos	Newmarket
Cilley, Cutten	Nottingham
Joseph	Nottingham
Clancy, Jeremiah	Portsmouth
Clap, Supply	Portsmouth

Clark, see also Clerrk.
Allex'dr	Londonderry
Benj.	Henniker
Benj.	Lee
Bunker	Packersfield
Caleb	Canaan
Cephas	Keene
Daniel, n.	Barrington
Daniel	Boscawen
Daniel	Brentwood
Daniel	Stratham
Eleazer	Claremont
Eleazer Jr.	Claremont
Ephraim	Deering
Henry	Candia
Ichabod	Allenstown

Clark - Cont'd	
Isaac	Keene
Isaac	Lee
Jacob	Barrington
Jacob	Epping
Jesse	Keene
John	Candia
John	Londonderry (2)
John	Sanbornton
John, n.	Stratham
Johnathan, n.	Barrington
Jonathan	Epping
Jon'a Jr.	Epping
Jona'th	Gilmanton
Jonathan	Meredith
Jonathan	Northwood
Joseph	Chester
Joseph	Hopkinton
Joseph	Portsmouth
Joseph	Sanbornton
Joseph	Stratham
Joseph Jr.	Stratham
Jos'h	Newmarket
Josiah	Nottingham
Josiah	Portsmouth
Matthew	Londonderry
Moses, n.	Stratham
Nathaniel	Brentwood
Nicholas	Sanbornton
Ninian, n.	New Boston
Richard	Canaan
Robert	Derryfield
Samuel	Brentwood
Sam'l	Epping
Samuel	Londonderry
Samuel, n.	Londonderry
Satchel	Sanbornton
Simeon Jr.	Keene
Solomon, n.	Rochester
Stephen	Candia
Stephen	Epping
Taylor	Stratham
Thos.	Amherst
Thomas	Portsmouth

Clark - Cont'd
William	Acworth
William	Henniker
William, n.	New Boston
William, n.	Newcastle
Will'm.	Nottingham
Clarke, Benj.	Epping
John	Portsmouth
Sam'l	Newcastle
Clarkson, James	Portsmouth
Clay, John	Candia
Cleaves, Nathan	Amherst

Clefford; see also Clifford.
David, n.	Brentwood
Isaac	Hawke
Samuel, n.	Brentwood
Clemens, James	Lee

Clement, Climent,
Christopher	Salem
Ezra	Weare
James	Dunbarton
Jesse	Weare
John	Atkinson
John	Hopkinton
John, n.	Salem
Jonathan	Bow
Jonathan	Weare
Nathaniel	Hopkinton
Paltiah	Bow
Sam'l, n.	Salem
William	Salem
Clements, Job	Rochester

Clendinin,
Andrew	Londonderry
David	Londonderry
Robt.	Londonderry
Clerrk, Amos	Hampstead

Clifford, Clafford; see also
Clefford.
Benjamin	Epping
Eben'r	Kensington
Ebenezer	Salisbury
Hezekiah	Epping
Israel	Dunbarton

Clifford - Cont'd
John	Candia
John Jr.	Kingston
Joseph	Gilmanton
Joseph	Kensington
Joseph	Kingston
Richard Jr.	Epping
Samuel	Boscawen
Samuel	Kensington
Stephen	Epping
Stephen	Kingston
Zechariah	Candia
Clough, Abner	Gilmanton
Abner	Nottingham
Benjamin	Kingston
Benjamin	South Hampton
Caleb	Northwood
Corneliush	Kingston
Daniel	Gilmanton
David	Gilmanton
David	Hopkinton
Elijah	East Kingston
Elisha	Bow
Elisha Jr.	Bow
Ezekiel	Epping
Ezekiel (Mr.)	South Hampton
Henry	Canterbury
Humphry	Sandown
Isaiah, n.	Gilmanton
James	Hopkinton
Jeremiah	Canterbury
John	Salem
Jonathan	Bow
Jonathan	East Kingston
Jonathan	Hawke
Jonathan	Loudon
Josiah	Salem
Leavitt	Canterbury
Nehemiah	Canterbury
Obadiah	Canterbury
Reuben	Sandown
Richard	Bow
Richard Jr.	Bow
Richard	Candia

Clough - Cont'd	
Samuel	Candia
Samuel	Gilmanton
Simon	Gilmanton
Theophilus	Candia
Thomas	Canterbury
Thomas Jr.	Canterbury
Timothy	Weare
William, n.	Salem
William Jr.	Salem
William	South Hampton
Winthrop	Weare
Zaccheus	Lee
Cloutman, Eliph	Barrington
John, Q	Rochester
Thomas, Q	Rochester
Clyd, Hugh	Windham
John	Windham
Joseph	Windham
Cobb, Daniel	Westmoreland
Ebenezer	Temple
Isaac	Westmoreland
Seth	Temple
Stephen	Temple
Cobleigh, Dan	Chesterfield
John	Chesterfield
Jonathan	Chesterfield (2)
Oliver	Chesterfield
Coburn, Amasa	Chesterfield
Amos	Wilton
Andrew	Chesterfield
Benjamin	Chesterfield
George	Wilton
Cochran, Elijah	New Boston
Isaac	Londonderry
Isaac	Windham
Jacob	Salisbury
James	Londonderry (2)
James, n.	Londonderry
James Jr.	Londonderry
James	New Boston
James Jr.	Pembroke
James 3d	Pembroke
James	Windham

Cochran - Cont'd	
John	Amherst
John	Londonderry
John, n.	New Boston
John Jr.	New Boston
John	Pembroke
John Jr.	Pembroke
John	Windham
John Jr.	Windham
Joseph	Londonderry
Joseph	Pembroke
Nathanel	New Boston
Ninian	New Boston
Peter, n.	New Boston
Robert	Londonderry
Sam'l	Londonderry
Thomas, n.	New Boston
William	Londonderry
Will'm	Pembroke
Codman, William	Amherst
Codmon, Henry	Amherst
Coffeen, Eliezre	Rindge
Coffin, Amos	Hampton
Enoch	Epping
Moses	Epping
Peter	Boscawen
Stephen	Conway
William	Concord
William	Epping
Coffrin,	
James (Leut.)	Pembroke
Cogin, Joseph	Amherst
Cogswell,	
Jeremy	Gilmanton
Nath'l	Atkinson
Colbath; see also Colebroth.	
Depandance	Barnstead
Joseph	Newington
Winthrop	Nottingham
Colbetat[?],	
Pilancon	Portsmouth
Colbey; see also Colby.	
Benjamin	Sandown
David	Londonderry

Colbey - Cont'd		Colby - Cont'd	
Elijah	Bow	Nathan	Salisbury
Jacob	Dunbarton	Nicholas	Hopkinton
James	Kingston	Orlando	Sandown
Jon'a. Sr.	Sandown	Peter	Sandown
Moses	Dunbarton	Samuel	Canterbury
Moses	Hawke	Thomas	Weare
Neamiah	Hopkinton	Willeby	Bow
Sargent	Dunbarton	William	Hopkinton
Colburn, Asa	Lebanon	Colcord, Daniel	Kingston
David	Lebanon	Ebenezer	Brentwood
Elias	Temple	Ebenezer Jr.	Brentwood
John	Lebanon	Edward	Newmarket
Stephen	Lebanon	Gideon	Newmarket
Colby, Coulby; see also Colbey.		Jonathan	Newmarket
Abner	Hopkinton	Joseph	Newmarket
Abraham	Bow	Josiah	Newmarket
Abraham	Conway	Samuel	Brentwood
Anthony	Hopkinton	Samuel	Kingston
Benaiah	Candia	Cole, Adam	Salem
Benjamin	Sanbornton	Amos, n.	Claremont
Daniel	South Hampton	Ebenezer	Richmond
David	Londonderry	John	Amherst
Eben	Sandown	John	Westmoreland
Edmon	Canterbury	Jonathan Jr.	Westmoreland
Eliphelet	Henniker	Jonathan 3d	Westmoreland
Eliphelet	Hopkinton	Nathan	Amherst
Enoch	Candia	Sam'l Esq., n.	Claremont
Ephraim	Salisbury	Solomon	Salem
Er	South Hampton	Colebroth,	
Hesekiah	Dunbarton	Hunking	Rochester
Isaac	Hopkinton	Coleman; see also Colman.	
Isaac	Sanbornton	Eleaz'r	Rochester
Jethro	Chester	Phinehas	Newington
John	Bow	Phinehas Jr.	Newington
John	Candia	Colis; see also Colles.	
John	Chester	Timothy Jr.	Weare
John	Sanbornton	Colleney, John	Keene
John	Sandown	Collens, Colens,	
John	Weare	John	Portsmouth
John Jr.	Weare	Jonathan	Kingston
Joseph	Concord	Collense, John Jr.	Newcastle
Joseph	Conway	Colles; see also Colis.	
Lot	Concord	Asa	Salem

Collet, John	Nottingham	Converce,	
Collines, Joseph	Monadnock	Sam'l Davis, n.	Chesterfield
Collins, Colings;	see also Collens	Converse, Robart	Monadnock
Benjamin	Canterbury	Cook,	
Daniel	Monadnock	Abraham	Rochester
Ebenezer	East Kingston	Ebenezer	Keene
Ebenezer	Hopkinton	Ebenezer	Wakefield
John	Salisbury	George	Richmond
John	Sandown	Jesse	Lebanon
Jonathan	East Kingston	John	Rochester
Joseph	Hawke	John	Wakefield
Rich'd	South Hampton	Josiah	Alstead
Robet	Sandown	Nathanael	Wakefield
Samuel, Q	Weare	Silas	Keene
William	Kingston	William	Richmond
Colman, see also	Coleman.	Cooke, John	Newmarket
James	Newington	Cooper, Aaron	Hinsdale
John	Newington	Benj.	Kingston
Joseph	Newington	Ebenezer, n.	Chesterfield
Colough, Joseph	Concord	John, s.	Croydon
Colwell,		John, n.	Croydon
William, n.	Lee	John Jr.	Croydon
Comins, Samuel	Hinsdale	John	Westmoreland
Comstock,		Nathaniel	Alstead
Azariah	Richmond	William	South Hampton
Azariah Jr.	Richmond	Copp, Benjamin	Conway
Moses	Richmond	David	Salem
Conant, Amos	Claremont	David	Wakefield
Roger	Westmoreland	Ebenezer	Hampstead
Conet, Joshua	Londonderry	Jonathan	Wakefield
Connelly, David	Londonderry	Solomon	Sanbornton
Conner, David	Pembroke	Copps, Benj.	Rochester
George, Q	Kensington	Moses	Wakefield
Connor; see also	O'Connor.	Corles; see also	Colis.
David	Hopkinton	Timothy	Weare
Ebenezer	Epping	Corlies,	
Jeremiah	Gilmanton	Nathaniel, n.	Weare
John	Pembroke	Corlis, Daniel	Salem
Morgan	Newmarket	James	Salem
Moses	Hopkinton	Jonathan	Salem
Philip	Meredith	Corliss,	
Samuel	Epping	Joshua, n.	Hampstead
Samuel	Pembroke	Corning, Gorg	Londonderry
Convarse, Zebulon	Rindge	John	Salem

Corser, Asa	Boscawen
David	Boscawen
John	Boscawen
John Jr.	Boscawen
Nathan	Boscawen
Thomas	Boscawen
Cory, Benoni	Conway
Coser, Jonathan	Boscawen
Samuel	Boscawen
Cossen,	
Ichabod, n.	Rochester
Joshua	Rochester
Cosset,	
Ranna (Rev) n.	Claremont
Cotton, Joseph	Portsmouth
Josiah	Sandown
Nathanel	Portsmouth
Thomas	North Hampton
Thomas	North Hampton
Thomas	Portsmouth
Thomas, n.	Sandown
William	Portsmouth
Wm. Jr.	Portsmouth
Couch, Benjamin	Boscawen
John	Boscawen
Coulby, see Colby.	
Coway, George	Bedford
Cox, John	Londonderry
Coy, William, n.	Claremont
Craford, John	Chester
Robert	Sandown
Crage, Allex'dr	Londonderry
David	Chester
Cragin, Benj.	Temple
Francis	Temple
John	Temple
John Jr.	Temple
Craig; see also Crage, Craige.	
Alexander	Londonderry
John	Wilton
Robert	Wilton
Craige, Creage, Creaig,	
David	Londonderry
John	Londonderry

Craige – Cont'd	
Robert	Chester
Robert	Londonderry
Thomas	Londonderry
Crain, Thomas	Richmond
Cram, Benj.	Exeter
Ebenezer	Wilton
Elijah	Seabrook
James	Newmarket
Jerediah	Weare
Joel	Deerfield
John	Deerfield
John	Wilton
John Jr.	Wilton
Jonathan	Salisbury
Jonathan	Wilton
Joseph	Deerfield
Joseph	Wilton
Nathan	Weare
Nathan Jr.	Weare
Nehemiah, n.	Deerfield
Sanborn	Deerfield
Wadleigh	Deerfield
Crane; see also Crain.	
Abia	Surry
Lemuel	Alstead
Creage, Creaig; see Craige.	
Creighton,	
Josiah	Exeter
Stephen	Brentwood
Cresey, Daniel	Hopkinton
Jonathan	Chesterfield
Joseph	Salem
Michael	Chesterfield
Richard, n.	Hopkinton
Crichet, Thomas	Sanbornton
Cristy,	
George, n.	New Boston
Jesse, n.	New Boston
Thomas	Londonderry
Crocker,	
Gershom	Gilsum
Crocket,	
Ephram	Stratham

Crocket - Cont'd	
Joshua	Meredith
William	Epping
Crockett, Chas	Epping
David	Stratham
John	Stratham
Crombey, Moses	Derryfield
Samuel	Chester
Crombie, Crumbie,	
Benjamin	Derryfield
James	Londonderry
James	Rindge
Jno.	Londonderry
Crook, Andrew	Piermont
Charles	Piermont
Thomas	Piermont
Crosbe, Jonathan	Meredith
Crosbie, John	Hampton
Crosby, Josiah	Amherst
Samson	Amherst
Crosfield, James	Keene
Cross, Abiel	Salem
Jesse	Canterbury
John	Canterbury
Peter	Nottingham West
Ralph	Bow
Robart	Epping
Stephen	Canterbury
Crosset, Joshua	Portsmouth
Crossfield, see Crosfield.	
Crown, John	New Boston
Crumbie, see Crombie.	
Cullimore, John	Pembroke
Cumings; see also Comins.	
David	Nottingham West
Ebenezer	Nottingham West
Eleaser	Londonderry
Eleazar	Nottingham West
Silas	Amherst
Cummings,	
Archilaus	Temple
Cuningham,	
James	Peterborough
Moses	Peterborough

Cuningham - Cont'd	
Sam'l	Peterborough
Thomas	Pembroke
Thomas	Peterborough
Cunningham,	
James, n.	Pembroke
Robert	Derryfield
Wm.	Londonderry
Currier, Abner	Unity
Barnard	South Hampton
Benj.	Chester
Benj., n.	Henniker
Calleb	Portsmouth
Challis	South Hampton
Charles	Gilmanton
Daniel	Deerfield
David	Chester
David	Windham
Dudley	Salem
Ezekiel	Hampstead
Ezra	East Kingston
Jacob, n.	East Kingston
Jacob	Hampstead
Jeremiah	East Kingston
John	Atkinson
John	East Kingston
John, n.	Hopkinton
John	Salem (2)
John	South Hampton
Joseph	Deerfield
Moses	Weare
Nathan	South Hampton
Nicholas	South Hampton
Reuben	Bow
Reuben	South Hampton
Richard	South Hampton
Sam'l	Hampstead
Sargent	Hopkinton
Stephen	Salem
Thomas	Portsmouth
Thomas	South Hampton
William	Concord
Curtice, Jacob	Amherst
Jacob Jr.	Amherst

Curtice - Cont'd
Joseph	Londonderry
Curtis, Amriah	Richmond
John	Winchester
Noah	Richmond
Samuel	Richmond
Curts, Danil	Claremont
Cutler, Solomon	Rindge
Cutter, A. R.	Portsmouth
Benj.	Temple
James	Rindge
Rich'd	Nottingham West
Richard	Portsmouth
Thomas, n.	Keene
Cutting, Daniel	Monadnock
Joseph	Monadnock
Cutts, Sam'l	Portsmouth
Daby, see Darby.	
Daggett, Nathanael	Westmoreland
Dakin, Ebenezer	Nottingham West
Justus	Nottingham West
Levi	Nottingham West
Dale, John	Wilton
John Jr.	Wilton
Timothy	Wilton
Dalling, Sam'l	Portsmouth
Dalton, Josiah	North Hampton
Mikel	Rye
Moses	Epping
Timothy	North Hampton
Dam, Eliphelet	Newington
John	Deerfield
Dame, Abner	Rochester
Benj., n.	Rochester
George	Portsmouth
Hunking	Lee
Issachar	Newington
Jabez	Rochester
John	Newington
Jonathan, Q	Rochester
Joseph	Newington
Joseph	Rochester
Levi	Deerfield
Moses	Lee

Dame - Cont'd
Theodore	Portsmouth
Timothy	Newington
Zebulon	Rochester
Damon, John	Amherst
Damrell, Joseph	Portsmouth
Dana, Jonathan	Lebanon
Joseph	Lebanon
William	Lebanon
Danels, Samuel	Sandown
Danford,	
Jedediah	Boscawen
Jonathan	Meredith
Sam'l	Boscawen
William	Boscawen
William Jr.	Boscawen
Danforth,	
Moses	Sanbornton
Simeon	Concord
Daniel, Danil,	
Clement	Barrington
Ephraim	Barrington
Jacob	Barrington
Jacob Jr.	Barrington
John	Barrington
Joseph	Barrington
Joseph Jr.	Barrington
Rubon	Portsmouth
Daniell,	
Eliphalet	Portsmouth
Sam'l	Pembroke
Daniels, Danils; see also Danels.	
David	Nottingham
Ebenezer	Surry
Increas	Chesterfield
John	Keene
Peletiah	Barrington
Reuben	Keene
Samuel	Keene
Samuel	Nottingham
Danielson,	
Charles	Barrington
James	Barrington
Livi	Barrington

		Davis – Cont'd	
Danly, John	Richmond	Asa	Nottingham West
Darbon; see also Dearbon.		Clement	Lee
John	Chester	Daniel	Portsmouth
Jonathan	Chester	Daniel	Rindge
Samul	Candia	Daniel	Sandown
Darborn,		Daved	Lee
James, n.	Stratham	Dudley	Barrington
Darby, Daby,		Ebenezer	Rindge
David	Westmoreland	Edmund	Portsmouth
Jacob	Chester	Eleazer	Leavitt's Town
Thomas	Chesterfield	Ephraim	Rye
Darlen, Thomas	Candia	Isaac	Chesterfield
Darling,		Isaac	Hopkinton
Abraham	Hawke	James	Barrington
Benjamin	Sanbornton	James	Chesterfield
Benj. B.	Hopkinton	James	Lee
Elialiakim	Rindge	John	Lee (2)
John	Hampstead	John	New Boston
John	Hopkinton	John	Portsmouth
Timothy	Hopkinton	Jonathan	Chesterfield
William	Hopkinton	Jonathan	Nottingham
Darrah, Arthur	Windham	Joseph	Hopkinton
James	Londonderry	? Joseph	Weare
Darte, Eliphalet	Surry	Moses	Epping
Joshua	Surry	Moses	Nottingham
Joshua Jr.	Surry	Moses, n.	Nottingham
Nathaniel	Surry	Nathel	Nottingham West
Thos.	Surry	Nathan	Boscawen
Dascombe,		Peter	Temple
James	Wilton	Phillip	Kingston
Davenport, John	Portsmouth	Randall	Rindge
Davidson; see also Davison;		Reuben	Barrington
David	Windham	Reuben	Kingston
George	Londonderry	Reuben	Wakefield
George	Windham	Richard	Rindge
James	Windham	Robert	Concord
John	Windham	Robert	Nottingham
Thomas	Peterborough	Samuel	Allenstown
Will'm	Londonderry	Sam'l	Boscawen
Davis, Davise, Daveas, Daves,		Samuel	Chester
Abner	Nottingham	Samuel	Epsom
Abraham	Hopkinton	Sam'l	Kingston
Amos	Chesterfield	Samuel	North Hampton
Amos	Rindge		

Davis - Cont'd

Simon	Chesterfield
Simon	Rindge
Simon Jr.	Rindge
Solomon	Nottingham
Thomas	Piermont
Thomas Jr.	Piermont
Thos	Rochester
Timothy	Barnstead
Webster	Kingston
William	Hopkinton
William	Loudon
William	Rindge
Zebulon	Rochester
Davison, David	Londonderry
Wm.	Rye

Dawson,

Timothy, n.	Londonderry
Day, Benjamin	Amherst
Benja	Boscawen
Ebenezer	Keene
Ezra	Richmond
John	Keene
Noah	Packersfield
Othniel	Richmond
Samuel	Salem
William	Westmoreland

Dean,

Benj. Woodbridge	Gilmanton
John	Rindge
Seth	Rindge
Dearben, Peter	Chester
Stephen	Chester

Dearbon; see also Darbon;

Daniel	Brentwood
Ebenezer	Chester
Edward	Deerfield
Henery	Hawke
Jeremiah	Kensington
John	Hampton
Joseph	Chester
Nathan	Kensington
Nathaniel	Canterbury
Samuel	Kensington

Dearbon - Cont'd

| Shubel | Canterbury |

Dearborn,

Benjamin	Epping (2)
Benjamin	Leavitt's Town
Dn'l.	North Hampton
Henary	Northwood
James	Newmarket
Jermiah	North Hampton
John	North Hampton
John	Stratham
Joseph	North Hampton
Josiah	Hampton
Josiah	North Hampton
Levi	North Hampton
Levi	Northwood
Nathaniel	Hampton
Phinehas	North Hampton
Reuben	North Hampton
Reuben Gove	North Hampton
Reuben Gove Jr.	" "
Ruben	North Hampton
Samuel	Epping
Samuel	North Hampton
Sharborn	Northwood
Simeon	Wakefield
Simon	Epping
Dearing, James	Rochester
Delan, Daniel	Barrington

Delaney,

Delavarn	Surry
Delono, Gideon	Alstead
Demary, John	Rindge

Demeret,

Joseph (Capt)	Northwood
Dempsey, Edward	Portsmouth
Denmore, Corniles	Lee
Dennent, John	Portsmouth
Dennet, George	Gilmanton
Jeremiah	Portsmouth
Nath'l	Portsmouth
Dennett, John	Portsmouth
Joseph	Allenstown
Dennie, Albert	Barrington

Densmore; see also Denmore,	Doak,
Dinsmoor, Dinsmore.	James Jr., n. New Boston
Elijah Lee	Doall, Will Portsmouth
Gersham Winchester	Dockam, Thomas Meredith
Dergien, see Durgin.	Dockham, John Meredith
Dewey, Ebenezer Gilsum	Dockum, Benj. Epping
Ebenezer Jr. Gilsum	Benjamin Jr. Epping
Elijah Lebanon	Cotton Stratham
Elijah Jr. Lebanon	Dodg, Geo. Portsmouth
Dickey, Dikey; see also Dicky.	Dodge,
Adam Bedford	Batholema Amherst
Adam Londonderry	Benj. Amherst
David Chester	Benj. New Boston
James Raby	David, n. Claremont
John Derryfield	Elijah Winchester
Mat'w Londonderry	Elijah Jr. Winchester
Robert Chester	Josiah Amherst
Robert Londonderry	Josiah Westmoreland
Sam'l Londonderry	Nehemiah New Boston
William Londonderry	Nicholas Londonderry
William Windham	Noah New Boston
Dickson, John Keene	Samuel, n. Amherst
Dicky, William Londonderry	Samuel Londonderry
Dimick, John Jr. Gilsum	William Winchester
Dimock, John Gilsum	Doe, Bradstreet Newmarket
Timothy Gilsum	John Newmarket
Dimond, Ephraim Londonderry	Jonathan Jr. Newmarket
Ezekiel Concord	Joseph Lee
Ezekel Jr. Concord	Joseph Newmarket
Isaac Epping	Nicholas Newmarket
Israel Hawke	Nicholas Jr. Newmarket
Dinsmoor, James Londonderry	Reuben Newmarket
James Windham	Zebulun Jr. Newmarket
John Windham	Zebulon 3d Newmarket
Robt. Windham	Dolbar, Nicholas Rye
William Windham	Dolbeer, Daniel Chester
Dinsmore; see also Denmore,	Dolber, Isariel Candia
Densmore.	Dole; see also Doall.
Abraham Temple	Isaiah South Hampton
Robert Chester	Jacob South Hampton
Samuel Chester	Stephen Atkinson
Zebadiah Temple	Stephen Jr. Atkinson
Dix, Eason Raby	Dollef, John Brentwood
Tim'y Bow	Dollof, David Brentwood

Dollof - Cont'd		Dow - Cont'd	
John	Conway	Jonathan	Lee
John Jr.	Conway	Jonathan	South Hampton
Josiah	Conway	Jonathan, Q	Weare
Nichelos	Brentwood	Joseph	Hampton
Thomas	Exeter	Joseph	Kensington
Dolly, Richard	Portsmouth	Josiah	Kensington
Donaldson, James	Londonderry	Nathan	Kensington
Donnough, Jefferry	Windham	Nath'el	Kensington
Donovan, John, n.	New Boston	Nath'l	Salem
Mathew, n.	New Boston	Noah	Gilmanton
Doolittle, Oliver	Hinsdale	Oliver	Hopkinton
Dorman, Ephraim	Keene	Percy	Salem
Doty, see Dutty, Duty.		Richard	Salem
Douglass, Thomas,		Richd. Jr.	Salem
(Deac'n), n.	Salem	Samuel	Bow
Dow,		Samuel	Hampton
Abraham	Salem	Samuel	Nottingham West
Amasa	Bow	Simon	Hampton
Amos	Salem	Thomas	Salem
Asa	Salem	Winthrop	Epping
Benaiah	Epping	Dowlin, William	Epping
Benj.	Epping	Downe,	
Benjamin	Gilmanton	William Jr.	Lebanon
Benjamin	Kensington	Downer,	
Daniel	Epping	William	Lebanon
Daniel	North Hampton	Zaccheus	Lebanon
David	Seabrook	Downing,	
Ebenezer	Epping	Bartholomew	Newington
Ela	Sandown	John	Newington
Gideon	Salisbury	Josh'a	Rochester
Isaac	Rye	Josiah	Newington
Isaac	Sandown	Rich'd	Newington
Jabez	Kensington	Rich'd Jr.	Newington
James	Atkinson	Sam'l, n.	Rochester
Jedidiah, Q	Weare	Downs, Gershom	Rochester
Jeremiah	Salem	James	Rochester
Jeremiah	Seabrook	Moses	Rochester
John	Atkinson	Dows, Jeptha	Westmoreland
John Jr.	Atkinson	Dowse,	
John	Hampton	Ozem Jr.	Rye
Jonathan	Brentwood	Dowst, Jon'a	Hampton
Jonathan	Gilmanton	Doyl, John	Westmoreland
Jonathan	Kensington	Doyne, Francis	Pembroke

Doyne - Cont'd	
Jacob	Pembroke
Drake, Dracke,	
Abraham	Brentwood
Abraham	North Hampton
Abraham Jr.	North Hampton
John	Hampton
John Jr.	Hampton
Robert	Hampton
Robert Jr.	Hampton
Samuel	Hampton
Samuel Jr.	Hampton
Simon	Epping
Thomas, n.	Epping
Thomas	Loudon
Weare	Leavitt's Town
Draper, Joseph	Sandown
Dresser, Asa	Hillsborough
Drew, David, n.	Barrington
John	Barrington
John	Loudon
Obediah	Barrington
Sam'l	Barnstead
Silas	Barrington
Thomas	Rochester
Drisco, James	Portsmouth
Drought, William	Epsom
Drown, Joseph	Rochester
Samuel	Rochester
Solomon	Rochester
Drowne, Peter	Newmarket
Sam'l	Portsmouth
Drury; see also Dury.	
Ebenezer	Temple
Gershom	Temple
Jonathan	Temple
William	Temple
Zedekiah	Temple
Duch, George	Lee
Ducky, John	Londonderry
Dudee, Zebulen	Newmarket
Dudley, Daniel	Gilmanton
Daniel	Newport
Ebenezer	Claremont

Dudley - Cont'd	
James	Brentwood
John	Brentwood
John Jr.	Brentwood
John	Gilmanton
John	Portsmouth
Jonathan S.	Newmarket
Joseph	Epping
Josiah	Brentwood
Josiah	Newport
Samuel	Brentwood (3)
Samuel Jr., n.	Brentwood
Stephen	Gilmanton
Winthrop	Brentwood
Dudly, Rauson	Brentwood
Samuel Paul	Hawke
Dufur, David	Monadnock
Dugan, Roger	Allenstown
Duncan,	
Abraham	Londonderry
George	Acworth
Georg	Londonderry
George Jr.	Londonderry
James	Society Land
John	Acworth
John	Londonderry (2)
John	Society Land
Josiah	Londonderry
Robert	Society Land
Wm.	Londonderry
Dunckle, David	Amherst
Duncklee, John	Amherst
Dunkley, Joseph	Amherst
Dunlap, Adam	Londonderry
James	Chester
Dunshe, Hugh	Londonderry
Durant,	
Jonathan, n.	Hillsborough
Durent, Samuel	Nottingham West
Durgan,	
Francis	Newmarket
Jacob	Newmarket
Durgen, James	Barrington
William, n.	Barrington

Durgin, Dergien,
Benjamin	Lee
Elijah	Hopkinton
Ephraim	Nottingham
Fraines Jr.	Newmarket
John	Northwood
Joseph	Canterbury
Joseph	Northwood
Josiah	Lee
Samuel	Lee
Will'm Jr.	Sanbornton
Duriell, G.	Portsmouth
Durkee, Nathan	Lebanon
Dury, John	Portsmouth

Dusten,
James, n.	Henniker
Paul	Weare
William	Weare
Dustin, David	Sanbornton
Eliphalet	New Boston
Duston, Caleb	Salem
Peter	Salem
Thomas	Claremont
Timothy	Claremont
Timothy	Salem
Dutch, see Duch.	
Dutton, Stephen	Westmoreland
Dutty, William	Londonderry
Duty, Moses	Windham
Dwinell, John	Londonderry
Jonathan	Keene
Stephen	Londonderry
Thomas	Keene
Dwyer, James	Portsmouth
Dyer, Samuel	Newmarket
William	Canterbury
Ealy, Enoch	Sanbornton
Eams, Ebenezer	Canaan
Earl, Esech, n.	Chesterfield

Easman; see also Esman, Esmon.
Ephraim	Kensington
Jeremiah	Deerfield
John, n.	Deerfield
Joseph	Hopkinton

Eastes,
Jonathan, Q	Weare

Eastman; see also Estam.
Abiather	Conway
Benj.	Concord
Benjamin	Hopkinton
Benjamin	Kensington
Daniel	East Kingston
Ebener	Gilmanton
Ebn'r.	Sanbornton
Edmund	Hampstead
Edward	Hawke
Edward	Salisbury
Enoch	Hopkinton
John	Kingston
Jonathan	Concord
Jonathan	Hampstead
Joseph	Boscawen
Joseph	Concord
Joseph Jr.	Concord
Joshua	Hampstead
Moses	Concord
Moses Jr.	Concord
Nicholas	Nottingham West
Obadiah	Salem
Peter	Hampstead
Philip	Concord
Richard	Concord
Richard	Conway
Samuel	Weare
Stephen	Bow
Stephen	Hopkinton
Timothy	Boscawen
William	Salisbury

Eastmen,
Benjamin	Hawke
Ebenezer	Kingston
Jacob	Hawke
Samuel	Hawke
Stephen	Hawke
Thomas	Hopkinton
Eaton, Benjiman	Seabrook
Benoni	Kingston
David	Seabrook

Eaton - Cont'd	
Ebenezer	Candia
Ephraim	Candia
Ephraim	Seabrook
Ezekiel	Sandown
Ithamar	Weare
Jabez	Hawke
Jabez	Seabrook
James	Candia
James	Hampstead
Jesse	Candia
John	Seabrook (2)
Joshua	Seabrook
Obadiah	Weare
Paul	Candia
Samuel	Seabrook
Thomas	Concord
Trustram	Seabrook
William	Candia
Wimon	Seabrook
Winthrop	Seabrook
Eatton, Eben'r	Atkinson
John	Hopkinton
Eayers; see also Eayrs, Eyers;	
James	Londonderry
Mark	Barrington
William	Londonderry
Eayrs, Christ'r	Acworth
Wm.	Londonderry
Eddy, Abiel	Westmoreland
James	Keene
Edgerley,	
David, n.	Gilmanton
Moses	Newmarket
Samuel	Brentwood
Edgerly,	
Benjamin	Barnstead
Jonathan	Meredith
Joseph	Brentwood
Joseph	Epping
Josiah	Epping
Zebulon	Epping
Edmands,	
Edward	Sandown

Edson,	
Ebenezer, n.	Claremont
Jonah	Westmoreland
Eills, John	Rindge
Elbridge,	
Nathaniel	Sandwich
Eliot, Edmund	Chester
John, n.	Portsmouth
Jonathan	Epping
Jonathan	Pembroke
Thomas	Boscawen
Elkins, Abel	Salisbury
David	Gilmanton
Henry	Hampton
Henry	Hawke
Henry	Rye
Jasper	Gilmanton
Jonathan	Hampton
Moses	Hampton
Moses	Salisbury
Nathaniel	Gilmanton
Peter	Hawke
Samuel	Rye
Thomas	Kingston
Thomas Jr.	Kingston
Ella, Samuel, n.	Londonderry
Ellingwood,	
Robert, n.	Salem
Elliot, Abraham	Portsmouth
Barnard	East Kingston
Benjamin	Concord
David	Bow
Francis	Amherst
John	Barnstead
John	Boscawen
John Jr.	Boscawen
Nicholes	Boscawen
Richard	Portsmouth
Robart	Boscawen
Ellis; see also Eills;	
Barnabas	Claremont
Benj.	Keene (2)
Caleb	Keene
Elisha	Keene

Ellis - Cont'd		Emerson - Cont'd	
Gideon	Keene	Richard	Londonderry
Gideon Jr.	Keene	Robert	Hampstead
Henry	Keene	Sam'l	Chester
John	Chesterfield	Samuel	Lee
John	Richmond	Smith	Lee
Jon'a	Rochester	Stephen	Weare
Joseph	Keene	Timothy	Nottingham West
Joseph Jr.	Keene	Timothy Jr.	Nottingham West
Joshua	Keene	Watts	Hampstead
Josiah	Keene	Webster, n.	Salem
Martin	Richmond	Emery, Amos	Dunbarton
Morris, n.	Rochester	Amos	Temple
Moses	Chesterfield	Anthony	Hampton
Simeon	Keene	Antony	Conway
Timothy	Keene	Benjamin	Atkinson
Timothy Jr.	Keene	Benj. Jr.	Atkinson
Timothy 3d	Keene	Benj.	Concord
Wm	Keene	Caleb	Weare
Will'm, n.	Rochester	Enoch	Conway
Ellison, Richard	Canterbury	Humphery	Conway (2)
Ellsworth, Aaron	Brentwood	Jacob	Pembroke
Jeremiah	Brentwood	John	Rindge
Olever	Claremont	Jonathan	Chester
Samuel	Brentwood	Joseph Jr.	Pembroke
Elmer, Hezekiah	Hinsdale	Joshua	Atkinson
Emerson,		Josiah	Sanbornton
Benjamin	Barnstead	Moses	Atkinson
Benj.	Hampstead	Noah	Exeter
Benj. Jr.	Hampstead	Salvenus	Weare
Caleb	Hampstead	Thomas	Candia
Charles	Derryfield	Thomes	Hampstead
Daniel	Croydon	Zechariah	Temple
Daniel	Monadnock	Emmons, Noah	Chesterfield
Ephrom	Weare	Emons, Abel	Chesterfield
Ithamar	East Kingston	Joseph	Weare
James	Weare	Esman, Ichabod	Nottingham West
John	Lee	Esmon, Thomes	Weare
Jonathan	Barnstead	Estabrook,	
Jonathan	Concord	Hobart	Lebanon
Joseph, n.	Lee	John	Packersfield
Marde	Weare	Nehemiah	Lebanon
Moses	Hopkinton	Sam.	Lebanon
Nath'l	Candia	Estam, Aaron, n.	Henniker

Estes, see Eastes.		Farnam - Cont'd	
Estey, Aaron	Rindge	Theadoer	Concord
Isaac	Keene	Farnham,	
Evans, Dan'l	Portsmouth	Timothy	Concord
Esarel	Weare	Farnsworth,	
John	Hinsdale	Samson	Raby
Medad	Hinsdale	Farnum; see also Farnam,	
Rich'd	Portsmouth	Farnham;	
Rob	Nottingham	Abner	Concord
Step'n	Portsmouth	Ben'a	Concord
Thomas	Weare	Benjamin	Conway
Uriel	Hinsdale	Daniel	Concord
Wm	Rochester	Eben	Concord
Zur	Chesterfield	Ebenezer	Conway
Evens, Abner	Gilmanton	Ephraim	Concord
Daniel	Gilmanton	Ephraim Jr.	Concord
Edmond	Barrington	Ephrm	Concord
Everett, John	Temple	John	Concord
Everit, Samuel	Packersfield	Joseph	Amherst
Ewer, Nathaniel	Newmarket	Joseph	Concord
Ewins, James	Londonderry	Joseph Jr.	Concord
Eyers; see also Eayers, Eayrs;		Josiah	Concord
Samuel	Londonderry	Josiah Jr.	Concord
Fabyan, Febbyan,		Stephen	Concord
John	Newington	Zebediah	Concord
Samuel	Newington	Farr,	
Samuel Jr.	Newington	Aaron	Chesterfield
Fairbank,		Abraham	Chesterfield
Sam'l	Chesterfield	Daniel	Chesterfield
Zenas	Chesterfield	David	Chesterfield
Fairwil; see also Farwell;		Ebenezer	Chesterfield
Absalom	Packersfield	Ephram	Chesterfield
Faklin, see Franklin.		Isaac	Chesterfield
Falch, Joseph	Seabrook	John	Weare
Samuel	Seabrook	Jon'a	Chesterfield
Fall, James	Portsmouth	Jon'a 2d	Chesterfield
Fallows, see Fellows.		Jonathan 3d	Chesterfield
Farington, see Farrington.		Jonathan 4th	Chesterfield
Farizel, Samuel	Henniker	Samuel	Chesterfield
Farley, Timothy	Packersfield	Sam'l Jr.	Chesterfield
Farmer, Edward	Nottingham West	Thomas	Chesterfield
Joseph	Derryfield	William Jr.	Chesterfield
Farnam, see also Farnum;		Farrar, Isaac	Meredith
Stephen	Amherst	Israel	Gilmanton

Farrington, Farington,
  Jeremiah   Conway
  Phinehas   Wilton
  Samuel   Hopkinton
Farwell; see also Fairwil.
  John   Packersfield
  Jonathan   Chesterfield
  Oliver   Chesterfield
  Richard   Packersfield
  William   Chesterfield
Fasset, Adonijah Winchester
  Samuel   Winchester
Faver, Timothy Londonderry
Favour, David Dunbarton
Fay, Moses Winchester
  Nathan   Alstead
  Sherebiah   Chesterfield
Febbyan, see Fabyan.
Feilds, Patrick Claremont
Felch, see Falch.
Felker, Charles Barrington
  Isaiah   Barrington
  Julius   Barrington
  Michal   Barrington
Fellews, Natthel Hawke
Fellows,
  Adonijah   Deerfield
  Benjamin   Candia
  David   Hopkinton
  Isaac   Hopkinton
  Isaac   Kensington
  Jeremiah   Kensington
  Jeremiah Jr. Kensington
  John   Salisbury
  John   Seabrook
  Joseph   Kingston
  Samuel   Hawke
  Thomas   Sandown
  Timothy   Sandown
Felt, Aaron Temple
  Jonathan   Packersfield
  Joshua   Temple
  Peter   Temple
Felton, John Monadnock

Fenton, Francis Piermont
Ferber, see Furber, Furbur.
Feren, see Ferren.
Fernald,
  Gilbert   Portsmouth
  Mark   Portsmouth
Ferren, Feren,
  John   Epping
  Moses   Portsmouth
  William   Sandown
Ferrin, Enos Weare
Ferrne,
  Jonathan   Epping
Field, Feid,
  Elohu   Winchester
  Gains   Winchester
  Irael   Winchester
  James   Monadnock
  Joshua   Winchester
  Moses D. Surry
  Waitstill Winchester
  Zachariah Winchester
Fields; see also Feilds;
  Thos   Keene
Fife, James Pembroke
  John   Pembroke
  Silas   Monadnock
  William   Pembroke
Fifeld,
  Benjamin Brentwood
  Dan'l.   Sanbornton
  John   Salisbury
  Stephen Brentwood
Fifield,
  Abraham Salisbury
  Benjam   Concord
  David   Gilmanton
  Ebenezer Kingston
  Edward East Kingston
  Edward Salisbury
  Hen'y   Hampton
  John Clefford Kingston
  Jonathan Epping
  Jonathan Salisbury

Fifield - Cont'd	
Joseph	Candia
Joseph	Salisbury
Joseph	Stratham
Obadiah Peters	Salisbury
Peter	Kingston
Sam'l	Gilmanton
Samuel	Kingston
Stephen	Candia
Stephen	Hampton
William	Concord
William	East Kingston
Finlay, Joseph	Londonderry
Fisher, Ichabod	Keene
Samuel	Londonderry
Thos	Barrington
Timothy	Croydon
William	Chesterfield
Fisk, Ebenezer	Epping
Ephraim	Concord
Jonathan	Lee
Samuel	Allenstown
William	Amherst
William Jr.	Amherst
Fitch, John	Rindge
Paul	Rindge
Fitts, Abra'm	Candia
Daniel (Cornet), n.	Sandown
Nathan	Chester
Nathaniel	South Hampton
Richard	South Hampton
FitzGerald, Gerald	Exeter
Fitzgerrald, Rich'd	Portsmouth
Flagg, Asa	Hinsdale
Gershom	Portsmouth
Sam'l	Hampstead
William	Hinsdale
Flanders, Flenders,	
Aaron, n.	Boscawen
Abner	Concord
Asa	Hawke

Flanders - Cont'd	
Barnard	South Hampton
Benjamin	Sandown
Benj.	Weare
Christopher, n.	South Hampton
Daniel	Hopkinton
David	Hawke
Emos	Boscawen
Ezekiel	Boscawen
Ezekiel	South Hampton
Isaac	Hawke
Isaiah, n.	South Hampton
Jacob	Boscawen
Jeremiah, n.	South Hampton
Jeremiah Jr., n.,	South Hampton
Jesse	Boscawen
Jesse Jr.	Boscawen
John	Boscawen
Jonathan	Kensington
Joseph	Boscawen
Josiah	South Hampton
Merrill	South Hampton
Moses	South Hampton
Nathaniel	South Hampton
Onesiphorus	Meredith
Parker	South Hampton
Philip	South Hampton (2)
Richard	Concord (2)
Richard Currier,	South Hampton
Thomas	Gilmanton
Timothy	South Hampton
Fleither, Deniel	Canterbury
Flenders, see Flanders.	
Fletcher,	
Ebenezer Jr., n.	Chesterfield
Elijah	Hopkinton
Robert	Temple
Samuel	Chesterfield
Fling, Anthony	Lee
Flint, Amos	Amherst
Amos Jr.	Amherst

Flint - Cont'd	
Jacob	Hillsborough
Joseph	Hopkinton
Nathan	Amherst
Flood, James	Monadnock
Mark	Weare
Moses	Weare
Fogg,	
Abner	North Hampton
Abner	" "
Ebenezer	Seabrook
James	Kensington
Jeremiah	Kensington
John	Hampton
Joseph	Kensington
Phinehas	Epping
Samuel	North Hampton
Seth	Epping
Seth	North Hampton
Stephen, n.	Kensington
William	Kensington
Foll[a]nbe,	
Thomas	Chester
Follet, Joseph	Lee
William	Packersfield
Follett, John	Lee
Folonsbury,	
Moses	Weare
Folsham, John	Meredith
Nicholas Carr	Meredith
Folsom, Foulsom, Fulsom,	
Abraham	Epping
Abraham, n.	Gilmanton
Abraham	Meredith
Andrew	Newmarket
Asa	Newmarket
Benjamin	Deerfield
Benj.	Newmarket
Daniel	Gilmanton
David	Epping
David	Newmarket
Edward	Newmarket
Israel	Epsom
Jeremiah	Newmarket

Folsom - Cont'd	
John	Newmarket (2)
John	Sanbornton
Jonathan	Gilmanton
Jonathan	Newmarket
Joseph	Newmarket
Josiah	Epping
Josiah	Exeter
Josiah	Rochester
Levi	Newmarket
Moses	Brentwood
Nath'l, n.	Deerfield
Nath'l	Portsmouth (2)
Peter	Lee
Peter	Newmarket
Simeon	Newmarket
Willyiam	Newmarket
Willieam Jr.	Newmarket
Foox, see Fox.	
Ford, Foord,	
James	Nottingham West
John	Nottingham
Noah	Piermont
Seth	Piermont
Forest, John	Canterbury
Forrest,	
John Jr.	Canterbury
William	Canterbury
Forrey, Sam'l	Meredith
Forsaith, see Forsith.	
Forse, Isaac	Chester
Isaac Jr.	Chester
Forsith, Forsaith,	
Jonathan	Chester
Matthew Jr.	Chester
William	Deering
Forss, Jacob	Epping
Forster, Asa	Canterbury
David	Canterbury
Jonathan	Canterbury
Samuel	Chester
Foss, Fose,	
David	Chester
Ephraim	Barrington

Foss - Cont'd		Foster - Cont'd	
George	Barrington	Jere—	Salem
Henry	Newcastle	Joshua	Temple
Hinkson	Barrington	Luke	Portsmouth
Isaac C.	Stratham	Moses	Pembroke
James	Barrington	Samuel	Stratham
Jeremiah	Barrington	Thomas	Meredith
Jeremiah	Newmarket	Fowle, Dan'l	Portsmouth
Job	Rye	Jacob	Londonderry
John	Canterbury	John	Concord
John	Stratham	Fowler, Jacob	Newmarket
Jonathan	Nottingham	John	Boscawen
Mark	Barrington	Josiah	Sandown
Mark Jr.	Barrington	Oliver	Boscawen
Nathan Jr.	Barrington	Philip	Newmarket
Nathaniel	Barrington	Simonds	Newmarket
Richard	Brentwood	Thomas Jr.	Chester
Samuel	Barrington	Fox, Foox,	
Samuel Jr.	Barrington	Edward	Gilmanton
Samuel Doust	Rye	Edward	Nottingham
Solomon	Barrington	Elijah	Lee
Stephen	Barrington	John	Gilmanton
Thomas	Barrington	Foye, John Jr.	Barrington
Thos.	Canterbury	Franch, see French.	
Thomas, n.	Nottingham	Franklin, Faklin,	
Timothy	Canterbury	Ichabod	Winchester
Wallis	Rye	Ichabod Jr.	Winchester
William	Barrington	James	Winchester
Fost, Benj.	Rochester	Nathan	Westmoreland
Benjamin Jr.	Rochester	Stephen	Winchester
Foster, Abiel	Canterbury	Frease, Jacob	Epping
Asa	Pembroke	Freeman,	
Asa Jr.	Pembroke	Benjamin	Winchester
Caleb	Pembroke	Dan.	Richmond
Daniel	Canterbury	Freese,	
David	Bow	Andrew	Deerfield
David	Keene	George	Hampton
David Jr.	Keene	Jacob Jr.	Epping
Ephraim	Bow	Joseph	Hampton
Henry	Winchester	Freeze,	
Hezekiah	Salisbury	Chase, n.	Portsmouth
Jacob	Temple	French, Freanch, Franch,	
James	Rochester	Abel	Loudon
James	Temple	Abel	South Hampton

[43]

French - Cont'd

Abraham	Kingston
Andrew	Stratham
Andrew Jr.	Stratham
Barzillai	Epping
Benjamin	Deerfield
Benjamin	East Kingston
Benjamin Jr.	East Kingston
Broadstreet	Rochester
Daniel	South Hampton
Daniel	Stratham
David	Kingston
David	Rochester
Ebenezer	Loudon
Ebenezer Jr.	South Hampton
Elihu	South Hampton
Elisha	Stratham
Enoch	Deerfield
Ephraim	Amherst
Ephraim	Claremont
Ezekiel	South Hampton
Ezra	Epping
Ezra	Hampstead
Gould	Epping
Green	Hopkinton
Henery	Hopkinton
Henry	Kingston
Henry	South Hampton
Henry Jr.	South Hampton
Jabez	Chester
Jacob	Seabrook
James	Boscawen
James	Rochester
James	South Hampton
John	Kingston
John	Packersfield
Jonathan	Hawke
Jonathan Jr.	Hawke
Joseph	Atkinson
Joseph	Epping
Joseph (Dcr.), n.,	Hampstead
Joseph Jr.	Hampstead
Joseph	Salisbury

French - Cont'd

Joshua	Deerfield
Joshua	East Kingston
Levi	Epping
Moses	South Hampton
Nath'l	Sandown
Nicholas	Candia
Obadiah	South Hampton
Samuel	Epping
Samuel	Kingston
Samuel	Loudon
Samuel	Nottingham West
Silas	Keene
Simon	Candia
Simon	Rochester
Stephen	Bedford
Timothy	Loudon
William	Lee
William	Stratham
William Jr.	Stratham
Frink, Elijah	Lempster
Thos.	Keene
Frisbee, James	Portsmouth
Frohock, Thomas	Meredith
Frost, Geo. Jr.	Newcastle
John	Portsmouth
Jonathan	Monadnock
Jos.	Newcastle
Joshua	Hinsdale
Michael	Portsmouth
Nathaniel	Lee
Fruland, Thomas	Northwood
Frye, David	Pembroke
Fryer, Will'm	Pembroke
Fugard, Samuel	Bedford
Fuller, Amasa	Claremont
Amos	Wilton
Benj.	Chester
Benj.	Lebanon
Benjamin P.	Enfield
David	Chester
David	Temple

Fuller - Cont'd	
Enoch	Wilton
James	Lebanon
John	Sandown
Jonathan	Claremont
Joshua	Surry
Joshua Jr.	Surry
Nathan	Amherst
Peter	Claremont
Fulton, Elisha	Amherst
Furber, Jethro	Newington
Nehemiah	Newington
Furbur, Benj.	Rochester
Eli	Lee
John	Barnstead
Joshua	Northwood
Levi	Newington
Rich'd	Rochester
Richard Jr.	Rochester
Samuel	Rochester
Thomas	Rochester
William	Newington
Furnald, Dimond	Lee
John	Portsmouth
Rendal	Portsmouth
Furneld, Amos	Lee
Furnil, Charls	Nottingham
William	Portsmouth
Furniss, Rob't	Portsmouth
Gage[?],	
Ephraim	Hopkinton
Gage, James	Amherst
John	Concord
John	Hopkinton
John Jr.	Hopkinton
Joshua	Saville
Solomon	Concord
Gail, Ebenezer	Chesterfield
Gains, George	Portsmouth
Thomas	Portsmouth
Gale; see also Gail;	
Amos	Alstead
Amos	Kingston
Bart	Exeter

Gale - Cont'd	
Daniel	Concord
Daniel	East Kingston
Dan'l	Sanbornton
Jacob	East Kingston
John	Salisbury
John	Sanbornton
Joseph	Epping
Stephen	Sanbornton
Wm.	Portsmouth
Galland, see Garland.	
Gallushee,	
Daniel	Weare
Galt; see also Gault;	
Thomas	Bedford
Gambell,	
William	Derryfield
Gansey, see Garnsey	
Gardner,	
Ezekiel	Canaan
Henry	Portsmouth
John	Bedford
John	Portsmouth
Sam'l, n.	Portsmouth
Wm.	Portsmouth
Gares, Edward	Boscawen
Garies, James	Boscawen
Garland, Galland,	
Benjamin	Rye
Daniel	Rochester
Dodovah	Rochester
Eben'r	Rochester
Jacob	Salisbury
John	Barrington
Jon'a	Hampton
Jonathan Jr.	Hampton
Joseph	Hampton
Joseph	North Hampton
Moses	Salisbury
Nathaniel	Kingston
Nath'l, n.	Rochester
Peter	Rye
Richard	Northwood
Simon	Rye

Garlen, John Jr.	Barrington
Garman, Joseph	Nottingham
Garnsey, Gansey,	
Amos	Richmond
John	Richmond
Oliver	Richmond
William	Richmond
Garrish, Paul	Nottingham
Garven, James	Bow
John	Bow
Patrick	Bow
Gary, Mosses	Unity
Gaskill, Jonathan	Richmond
Silas	Richmond
Gates, Daniel, n.	Westmoreland
Elias	Westmoreland
Isaac	Henniker
Gault; see also Galt;	
Andrew	Pembroke
Samuel	Pembroke
William	Canterbury
Gay,	
Bunker (Rev.)	Hinsdale
Jacob	Allenstown
Geeir, Benajah	Hinsdale
George, Gorge,	
Austin	Hampstead
David	Concord
Enos	South Hampton
Gideon	Kingston
Isaac	Sandwich
John	Hopkinton
Joseph	Derryfield
Joseph	Weare
Joshua	Sandown
Josiah	Leavitt's Town
Thomas	Dunbarton
Thomas	Nottingham
Timothy	Weare
William	Hampstead
Geris; see also Gares, Garies;	
Samuel	Amherst
Gerrish; see also Garrish;	
Enoch	Boscawen

Gerrish - Cont'd	
Henry	Boscawen
Joseph	Boscawen
Samuel	Canterbury
Stephen (Capt.)	Boscawen
Stephen	Boscawen
Getchel,	
Zebulun	Dunbarton
Gibbs,	
Joseph, n.	Temple
William	Portsmouth
Gibson, Abel	Henniker
Daniel	Hillsborough
James	Sanbornton
John	Canterbury
John	Hillsborough
Thomas	Canterbury
Timothy	Henniker
Tim'o Jr.	Henniker
Giddinge,	
Eliphalet	Exeter
John	Exeter
John Jr.	Exeter
Giden, Simeon	Unity
Giffen, Robert	Bedford
Giffers, John	Hampstead
Gilbert, Gideon	Westmoreland
Seth	Westmoreland
Gilchrist; see also Gillchrest;	
William	Chester
Gilcrest,	
William	Chester
Gile; see also Guile;	
James	Hampstead
John	Nottingham
Johnson	Hopkinton
Noah, n.	Henniker
Giles, Benj.	Newport
John	Londonderry
John	Nottingham
Nicholas	Sanbornton
Ruel	Lee
Samuel	Stratham
Gill, William	Epping

Gill – Cont'd	
William	Nottingham

Gillchrest; see also Gilchrist;

Richard	Dublin
Gillmor, James	Bedford
Jonathan	Londonderry
Whitefield	Bedford

Gillmore; see also Gilmore;

| James | Amherst |

Gilman, Gillman,

Andrew	Newmarket
Andrew	Wakefield
Antipas	Gilmanton
Antipasse, n.	Brentwood
Benjamin	Gilmanton
Brads.	Epping
Bradst.	Newmarket
Caleb	Sanbornton
David	Exeter
Edward	Gilmanton
Eliphelet	Gilmanton
Ezekiel	Deerfield
Ezekiel	Pembroke
Iseriel	Sandwich
James	Newmarket
Jeremiah	Wakefield
Jeremiah Jr.	Wakefield
John	Epping
John	Gilmanton
John	Kingston
John	Londonderry
John	Wakefield
Jonathan, n.	Gilmanton
Jonathan Jr.	Gilmanton
Jonathan 3rd	Gilmanton
Jonathan	Wakefield
Jonathan Jr.	Wakefield
Joseph	Exeter
Joseph	Newmarket
Joseph	Sanbornton
Joshua	Gilmanton
Josiah Jr.	Exeter
Josua	Gilmanton
Jotham	Gilmanton

Gilman – Cont'd	
Moses	Sanbornton
Nathaniel	Brentwood
Nath'l	Newmarket
Nath'l	Pembroke
Peter	Gilmanton
Peter Jr.	Pembroke
Samuel	Deerfield
Samuel	Gilmanton
Sam'l	Newmarket
Samuel, n.	Newmarket
Samuel Folsom	Exeter
Simon	Brentwood
Summersbee	Gilmanton
Thos.	Canterbury
Wm. Jr.	Loudon
Wintrop	Gilmanton
Zebulun	Exeter

Gilmore; see also Gillmor(e);

James	Windham
Robert, n.	Keene
Robert	Londonderry
William	Londonderry
Gipson, James	Canterbury
Glasier, David	Westmoreland
Glass, James	Nottingham

Gleason, Glesen,

Benjamin	Westmoreland
Bezaleel	Croydon
Fortunatus	Westmoreland
James	Westmoreland
Job	Surry
Job Jr.	Surry

Gleeson,

| Timothy | Barrington |

Glidden, Gliden, Gleden,

Andrew	Gilmanton
Andrew	Unity
Jeremiah, n.	Deerfield
John	Sandwich
Jonathan, n.	Unity
Joseph	Unity
Nathanel	Chester
Rich'd, n.	Unity

Glidden - Cont'd	
Robert	Gilmanton
William	Lee
Glines, James	Canterbury
John	Loudon
Nathaniel	Canterbury
Richard	Canterbury
William Jr.	Canterbury
Glover, David	Nottingham West
John	Lee
Richard, n.	Lee
Goddard,	
William	Richmond
William, n.	Westmoreland
Godding, Henry	Rindge
Godfree, John	Deerfield
Jonathan	Hampton
Moses	Northwood
William	North Hampton
Godfrey, James	North Hampton
William	Hopkinton
Goen, William	Lee
Goffe, John	Bedford
John Jr.	Bedford
John	Derryfield
Goldsmith,	
William	Wilton
Gooch, Jam's.	Portsmouth
John	Portsmouth
Goodale, Enos	Temple
Ezekiel	Temple
Gooden, James	Claremont
Goodenogh,	
William	Keene
Goodenough,	
Jonathan	Westmoreland
Goodenow, Asa	Westmoreland
Benjamin	Monadnock
Daniel	Monadnock
Edmund	Westmoreland
Isreal	Westmoreland
Jonathan	Monadnock
Naham	Westmoreland
Goodhue, Samuel	Deerfield

Goodhue - Cont'd	
Nathaniel, n.	Nottingham
Goodridge,	
Allen	Amherst
Goodwin, Benj.	Epsom
Edward	Claremont
Jacob	Concord
James	Newmarket
Robert	Newmarket
Samuel	Concord
Samuel	Stratham
Theo's	Dunbarton
Thomas	Claremont
Timothy	Hampstead
Gookin,	
Nathaniel	Boscawen
Nat'h.	Portsmouth
Goold, Abijah	Temple
Ambrose	Pembroke
Amos	Henniker
Richard	Amherst
Gorden, Abner	Hopkinton
Alexander	Salem
Ellxandor	Loudon
John	Hampstead
Jonathan	Brentwood
Jonathan	Hopkinton
Jonatham	Salem
Nath'l	Exeter
Phinehas	Salem
Scribner	Brentwood
Thomas	Boscawen
Thomas	Brnetwood
Timothy	Brentwood
Gordon, Amos	Brnetwood
Daniel	Epping
Daniel	Salem
John, n.	New Boston
Robert	Chester
William	Salem
Gordy, Maseck	Sandown
Gorge, William	Hawke
Gorman; see also Garman;	
James	Derryfield

Gorrell, Nath'l	Salem
Goss, James	Rye
John	Claremont
Jonathan	Rye
Levi	Rye
Nathan	Rye
Nathanell	Claremont
Philip	Winchester
William	Hinsdale
Gouch, Stephen	Nottingham West
Goudy; see also Gowdy;	
Thomas	Newcastle
Goul, Nathan	Weare
Gould; see also Goold;	
Benjamin	Rindge
Christopher, n.	Hopkinton
Daniel	Weare
Gideon	Hopkinton
Jacob	Rindge
John	Dunbarton
John, n.	Winchester
Joseph	Amherst
Joseph	Nottingham West
Moses	Hopkinton
Muzzey, Q	Rochester
Nathan, n.	Hopkinton
Oliver	Rindge
Thomas, n.	Winchester
Gouler, Mich'l	Portsmouth
Gove, Abraham	Deering
Abraham	Kensington
Daniel, Q	Weare
Eben'r	Sanbornton
Elijah	Weare
Elisha, Q	Weare
Enoch	Seabrook
John, Q	Weare
John Jr., Q	Weare
Jonathan, n.	New Boston
Jonathan	Nottingham
Jonson, Q	Weare
Joseph	Seabrook
Nathan	Seabrook
Nathaniel	Kensington

Gove - Cont'd	
Obadiah, Q	Kensington
Samuel, n.	Nottingham
Stephen, Q	Weare
Winthrop	Seabrook
Gow, Nathaniel	Kensington
Gowdy; see also Goudy;	
Wliam	Newcastle
Gowing, Timothy	Deerfield
Grag, Gragg, see Gregg.	
Graham, Greaham,	
George	Concord
George	Derryfield
Hugh	Windham
Hugh Jr.	Windham
John	Hillsborough
Grahames,	
Robert	Chester
Grandey, John	Chesterfield
John Jr.	Chesterfield
Robert	Hinsdale
Granis,	
Timothy, n.	Claremont
Grant, Daniel	Exeter
Daniel	Portsmouth
John	Portsmouth
Graves, David	South Hampton
Jacob	East Kingston
Jacob	Weare
John	Kensington
Joseph	Deerfield
Nathaniel	Brentwood
William	Brentwood
William Jr.	Brentwood
William	South Hampton
Gray, Aaron Jr.	Keene
James	Barrington
James	Dunbarton
Jeremiah	Barrington
John	Barrington
John	Lebanon
John	Rindge
Kalso	Peterborough
Mathew	Chesterfield

Gray - Cont'd		Green - Cont'd	
Robert	Peterborough	John, Q	Kensington
Ruben	Barrington	John	Society Land
Samuel	Barrington	Jonathan, Q	Kensington
Samuel	Nottingham	Joseph	Atkinson
Timothy	Wilton	Micah, Q	Weare
Timothy Jr.	Wilton	Nathan	Seabrook
William	Barrington	Nath'l	Concord
William Jr.	Barrington	Nathaniel	Deerfield
William	Keene	Peter Jr.	Concord
William	Londonderry	Stephen, Q	Kensington
Greaham, see Graham.		Greene, Daniel	Richmond
Greele, Grele,		Peter	Concord
Benjamin	Salisbury	Greenfield,	
Ezekiel	Londonderry	Bennet	Kingston
Jonathan	Wilton	Greenlaw,	
Nathaniel	Wilton	Alexander	Portsmouth
Reuben	Salisbury	Greenleaf, Jn'o.	Portsmouth
Richard	South Hampton	Paul	Seabrook
Sam'l	Nottingham West	Stephen	Concord
Sam'l Jr.	Nottingham West	Greenough,	
Shubael	Salisbury	Daniel	Chester
Greeley, Aaron	Hopkinton	Moses	Atkinson
Andrew	East Kingston	Richard	Dunbarton
Edward	East Kingston	Greenwood,	
Jonathan	East Kingston	Eli	Dublin
Jonathan (Col.), n.,		Joseph	Dublin
	East Kingston	Josiah	Dublin
Jonathan Jr.	East Kingston	Moses	Dublin
Moses	East Kingston	William	Dublin
Philip	Hopkinton	Greg, John	Londonderry
Samuel	Gilmanton	Gregg, Gragg, Grag,	
Greely,		Adams	Peterborough
Joseph, n.	Brentwood	Alex'r	New Boston
Green, Amos	Amherst	Alexander Jr. (E'n),	
Asahel	Seabrook		New Boston
Benjamin	Stratham	Alexander	Windham
David	Amherst	Benjamin	Londonderry
Eben'r	Atkinson	Daniel	Rindge
Elijah	Weare	David	Windham
Isiah, Q	Weare	David Jr.	Windham
Isiah Jr., Q	Weare	George	Londonderry
Jacob	Concord	Hugh, n.	New Boston
Jeremiah, Q	Weare	James	Londonderry

Gregg - Cont'd	
James	New Boston
James	Society Land
James Jr.	New Boston
John	Peterborough
John Jr.	Peterborough
Joseph	Londonderry
Lessly	New Boston
Samuel	Londonderry
Samuell	Londonderry
Samuel	Peterborough
Thomas	Piermont
Thomas	Windham
William	Londonderry
Will'm	Windham
Will'm Jr.	Windham
Gregory, John	Portsmouth
Grele, see Greele.	
Grendel, Daniel	Saville
Grifeen,	
Eliphelet Jr.	Deerfield
John	Deerfield
Nathan	Deerfield
Grifen, Grefin,	
John	Derryfield
Moses	Sandown
Peter	Sandown
Richard	Sandown
Theoffles	Derryfield
Theophilus	Sandown
Thomas	Sandown
Griffen,	
Domenikes	Deerfield
Eliphelet	Deerfield
James	Deerfield
Joseph	Derryfield
Theoph's	Deerfield
Griffing, Ebenezer	Kingston
Griffith,	
Nathaniel S.	Portsmouth
Grimes, Ghrims,	
Bartholomew	Keene
Frances	Deering
James	Deering

Grimes - Cont'd	
James	Wilton
John	Amherst
John	Chester (2)
Jonathan	Amherst
Samuel	Londonderry
William	Londonderry
William	Wilton
Griswold,	
Jeremiah	Lebanon
John	Lebanon
Oliver	Lebanon
Stephen	Gilsum
Gross, John	Chester
Grouard, James	Portsmouth
Grout,	
Jehoshaphat	Rindge
Grover, Amaziah	Alstead
Grushe, John	Bow
Guild, Dan	Keene
Guile; see also Gile;	
Asa	Nottingham
Jonathan	Canterbury
Gummer,	
Ezekiel	Portsmouth
Gunnison, John	Portsmouth
Samuel	Saville
William	Portsmouth
Gunson, John	Londonderry
Hacket,	
Jeremiah	Canterbury
Josiah	Westmoreland
Hadley; see also Hadly;	
Daniel	Weare
Eliphalet Jr.	Nottingham West
Ezekiel	Hopkinton
George, n.	Weare
Moses	Nottingham West
Nehemiah	Windham
Parrit	Nottingham West
Samuel	Hopkinton
Stephen	Nottingham West
Hadlock, James	South Hampton
Jonathan	Weare

Hadlock - Cont'd	
Joseph	Weare
Joseph Jr.	Weare
Levi	South Hampton
Hadly, Eliphalet	Nottingham West
Seth	Nottingham West
Hager, Amos	Croydon
Hagget, Josiah	Pembroke
Hailey, see Hayley.	
Haines; see also Hanes;	
Abner	Canterbury
Cotton	Deerfield
David	Deerfield
Joseph	Wakefield
Josiah	Portsmouth
Samuel	Canterbury
Samuel	Wakefield
Walter	Canterbury
William	Deerfield
Hains, John	Gilmanton
Joshua	North Hampton
Hale, Benj.	Atkinson
David	Rindge
Enoch	Rindge
Henery	Nottingham West
Henery Jr.	Nottingham West
John	Boscawen
John	Nottingham West
Joseph	Atkinson
Moses	Alstead
Moses	Rindge
Sam'l (Maj'r), n.	Portsmouth
Hall, Abijah	Croydon
Amos	Newport
Avery	Rochester
Benjamin Jr.	Barrington
Caleb	Chester
Daniel	Concord
Daniel	Derryfield
Daniel	Wakefield
David	Concord
David, n.	Salem
Ebene'r	Concord
Ebenezer	Windham

Hall - Cont'd	
Edward, n.	Croydon
Henry	Chester
Isaac	Barrington
Jacob	Croydon
James	Salem
Jessey	Keene
John	Barrington
John	Derryfield
John (Deac'n), n.	Salem
Jonathan	Chester
Joseph	Barrington
Joseph	Concord
Joseph Jr.	Concord
Joseph	Croydon
Joseph	Rye
Joshua Jr.	Barrington
Joshua	Salem
Josiah	Chester
Nathaniel	Candia
Nathaniel	Lebanon
Nathaniel	Nottingham
Obadiah	Candia
Obadiah	Concord
Obededom	Candia
Peter	Chester
Ralph	Barrington
Rapha	Salem
Sam'l	Keene
Sam	Portsmouth
Samuel	Wakefield
Sam'l R'd	Croydon
Solomon	Barrington
Timothy	Wilton
Will.	Raby
William	Salem
Halle,	
Benjamin (Lt.), n.	Keene
Hals, Nathaniel	Londonderry
Ham, Aaron	Rochester
Benson	Epsom
David	Wakefield
Eph'm.	Portsmouth
Ephraim	Rochester

Ham - Cont'd		Hardey, David	Dunbarton
George	Barrington	Hardie, Biley	Kingston
Gorge	Portsmouth	Nichlous	Brnetwood
Gideon	Deerfield	Hardy,	
John	Barrington	Bradbury	Seabrook
John	Rochester	Daniel	Nottingham West
John Jr.	Rochester	Jacob	Salem
Jon'a	Rochester	Jonathan Jr.	Nottingham West
Joseph	Portsmouth	Jonathan	Seabrook
Sam'l	Portsmouth (2)	Josiah	Salem
Samuel Jr.	Portsmouth	Nath'l	Nottingham West
Thomas	Rochester	Richard	Nottingham West
Timothy	Portsmouth	Robert	Wakefield
William	Barrington	Samuel	Deerfield
William	Portsmouth	Samuel	North Hampton
William Jr.	Portsmouth	Stephen, n.	Newmarket
Wm.	Rochester	Thomas	Bow
Hamblet, Thos.	Nottingham West	Hariess,	
Hammell, Joseph	Peterborough	Joseph	Salem
Neal	Peterborough	Hariman, see Harriman.	
Hammett, John	Rochester	Harkness, Nathan	Richmond
Moses	Rochester	Harper,	
Hammond, Abel	Winchester	John Scribner	Brentwood
Simpson	Richmond	Sam'l	Acworth
Hanaford, Hannaford,		Samuel	Brentwood
Benjamin	Concord	Samuel	Sanbornton
David	Stratham	Harriman, Hariman,	
John	Rindge	Gasiel	Chester
Peter	Canterbury	John	Hampstead
Thomas	Newmarket	John Jr.	Hampstead
Hanagan[?],		Joshua	Sandown
James	Epping	Leonard	Bow
Hancock, William	Canterbury	Leonard	Conway
Handsom, John	Rindge	Nathanel	Conway
Handy, Paul	Richmond	Reuben	Hampstead
Haneis, John	Epsom	Stephen	Hopkinton
Hanes, David	Epping	Thos	Hampstead
Richard	Canterbury	Harrington,	
Hans, Nathaniel	North Hampton	Jonah	Monadnock
Hanson,		Harris; see also Hariess;	
Aaron, n.	Lee	Anthony	Richmond
Jacob	Rochester	David	Keene
Tobias	Wakefield	Sam'l	Amherst
Harbert, Richard	Concord	Sam'l	Exeter

Harris - Cont'd		Harwood, John	Amherst
Samuel	Hopkinton	Haseltine,	
Thomas	Chesterfield	Asa	Atkinson
Uriah	Richmond	Daniel	Salem
Harrold, Jas.	Conway	John	Nottingham West
Robt.	Conway	John Jr.	Nottingham West
Hart, Balch	Wilton	Joseph	Concord
Daniel	Portsmouth	Nathaniel	Amherst
Edward	Portsmouth	Hash,	
George, n.	Newmarket	William, n.	Stratham
George	Portsmouth	Haskell, Abijah	Rindge
George Jr.	Portsmouth	John	Chesterfield
Henry	Newington	Haslett, James	Portsmouth
James	Portsmouth	Matthew	Portsmouth
John	Newington	Hassall, Elias	Deering
John Jr.	Portsmouth	Hasseltine; see also Haseltine,	
Jno. 3d	Portsmouth	Hazeltine, Heselton,	
Nathaniel	Newington	Hesseltine;	
R'd	Portsmouth	Benjamin	Chester
Robert	Portsmouth	John	Chester
Thos.	Portsmouth	Moses	Chester
William	Portsmouth	Peter	Chester
William, n.	Portsmouth	Richard	Chester
Hartford, Mark	Rochester	Sam'l	Chester
Nicholas	Newmarket	Thomas	Chester
Harthorn,		Hastinges,	
Ebenezer	Henniker	James	Salem
Hartshorn,		James Jr.	Salem
James	Amherst	Hastings,	
James	Lebanon	Andrew	Chesterfield
John	Amherst	Joseph	Hopkinton
Jonathan	Wilton	Joseph Stacy, n.	Portsmouth
Harvey, Ezra	Keene	Josiah	Chesterfield
Frances, n.	Nottingham	Robert	Canterbury
Frances Jr., n.	Nottingham	Thaddues	Monadnock
John	Derryfield	Hatch, Hosea	Gilmanton
John	Nottingham	[?] Jeremiah	Winchester
Levi	Deerfield	Joseph	Alstead
Nicholas	Newmarket	Phinehas	Alstead
Rich'd	Portsmouth	Hath, Jacob	Canterbury
Thomas	Nottingham	Haven, Joseph	Rochester
Thomas	Surry	Sam'l.	Portsmouth
Harvy, John	Nottingham	Sam'l. Jr.	Portsmouth
Phillip	Epping	Havery, Isaiah	Loudon

Hawkens,	
Stephen	Wakefield
Hayes; see also Hays;	
Aaron	Nottingham
Benjamin	Barrington
Benj.	Rochester
Daniel	Rochester
Hezekiah	Barrington
Ichabod	Rochester
James	Barrington
John	Allenstown
Joseph	Barrington
Joseph	Rochester
Moses	Rochester
Moses Jr.	Rochester
Paul	Barrington
Samuel	Barrington
Wentworth	Rochester
William Jr.	Sanbornton
Hayley, Thos.	Portsmouth
Hays, William	Barrington
Hayward, Nathan	Surry
Peter	Surry
Willim	Surry
Hazeltine,	
Barnes	Conway
James	Concord
Rich'd	Concord
William	Concord
Head, James	Pembroke
John	Pembroke
Nath'l	Pembroke (2)
Richard	Pembroke
Heald, Ephraim	Temple
Joseph	Temple
Oliver	Temple
Peter	Temple
Healey,	
Denis	Londonderry
Nath'l	Kensington
Healy, Helhay,	
John	Winchester
Nehemiah	Winchester
Sam'l	Winchester

Heard; see also Hurd;	
Benj., n.	Rochester
John	Rochester
Joseph, n.	Rochester
Reuben	Rochester
Reuben Jr.	Rochester
Tristram, n.	Rochester
Heath, Hethe,	
Asa	Sandown
Asa, n.	Weare
Bartho.	Hampstead
Benjamin	Canterbury
Caleb	Canterbury
Ephraham	Salisbury
Job	Salisbury
Joshua	Conway
Joshua	Henniker
Joshua, n.	Salem
Moses	Sandown
Richard	Hampstead
Serjant, n.	Henniker
Simeon	Bow
Solomon	Bow
William	Henniker
Heaton,	
Jonathan	Keene
Seth	Keene
Seth Jr.	Keene
Hebard; see also Hibbard;	
James	Lebanon
Moses	Lebanon
Hebbard,	
Jedidiah	Lebanon
Heely, Paul	Chester
Hellese, Robert	Deerfield
Hemphell,	
Joseph	Pembroke
Hemphill, Henry	Bow
John	Bow
Nathaniel	Windham
Nath'l Jr.	Windham
Robert	Windham
Henderson, Handerson,	
David, n.	New Boston

Henderson - Cont'd	
Hugh	Portsmouth
Hendrason,	
Joseph	Stratham
Hennesee,	
Richard	Salem
Henry, Samuel	Amherst
William	Chesterfield
Heramon,	
Eben'r (Ens'n), n.	Henniker
Hersey, Hearsey, Hearsee,	
John	Sandown
Peter, n.	Newmarket
Samuel	Sandown
Hervey,	
Ebenezer, n.	Chesterfield
Heselton, Joseph	New Boston
Hesseltine,	
Jonathan	Salem
Jonathan Jr.	Salem
Nathan	Wilton
Nath'n.	Wilton
Hibbard; see also Hebard, Hebbard;	
Augusten (Rev.)	Claremont
Hichcock; see also Hitchcock;	
John, n.	Claremont
Hickes, Pery	Barrington
Hickey, James, n.	Portsmouth
Hidden, Eben	Boscawen
James	Chester
Jere'h	Boscawen
Higbee, Chearles	Claremont
Stephen	Claremont
Higgans, John	Winchester
Higgins, Joseph	Chesterfield
Hight, Dennis	Portsmouth
James	Portsmouth
Joseph	Newington
Hiland, John	Londonderry
Hilands, Thomas	Londonderry
Hildreth, Asa	Hopkinton
David	Amherst
Edward	Chesterfield
Ephraim	Amherst

Hildreth - Cont'd	
Isaac	Chesterfield
Jacob	Amherst
Jonathan (Capt.), n.,	
	Chesterfield
Jonathan Jr.	Chesterfield
Samuel	Chesterfield
William	Chesterfield
Hill, Benj.	Northwood
David	Candia
Ebenezer	Dublin
Edward	Lee
Elisha	Portsmouth
James	Newmarket
James	Portsmouth
Jethro	Candia
John	Alstead
John	Barrington
John, n.	Stratham
Jonathan (Dr.), n.	Deerfield
Reuben	Lee
Robert	Northwood
Samuel	Lee
Samuel	Portsmouth
Timothy	Amherst
Volintine	Nottingham
Hillard,	
Jo Chase	Kensington
Joseph	Kensington
Hillery, John	Bedford
Hills; see also Hellese;	
Abner	Chester
Benj.	Chester (2)
Elijah	Nottingham West
Ezekiel	Nottingham West
Isaac	Chester
Jacob	Chester
Jeremiah	Nottingham West
John	Candia
John	Wakefield
Jonathan	Candia
Joseph	Chester
Joseph	Stratham
Moses	Chester

Hills – Cont'd	
Moses	Hopkinton
Olliver	Nottingham West
Philip	Nottingham West
Samuel	Chester
Samuel	Nottingham West
Stephen	Chester
Thomas	Nottingham West
William	Candia
William	Nottingham West
Hilton, Daniel	Newmarket
Edward Jr.	Newmarket
Henery, n.	Hampstead
Ichabod	Newmarket
Jeremiah	Sandwich
Joseph	Deerfield
Josiah	Newmarket
Sam'l, n.	Salem
Winthrop	Newmarket
Hinds, Ambros	Gilmanton
Hines,	
Thomas, n.	Nottingham
Hinkson, Samuel	Concord
Hitchcock; see also Hichcock;	
Ichabod	Claremont
Hitchings,	
Josiah	New Boston
Hix, Amos	Richmond
Barnard	Richmond
David	Richmond
Ephrm	Richmond
Oliver	Richmond
Samuel	Richmond
Hixson, Ebenezer	Monadnock
Hoag, Joseph, n.	Stratham
Nathan, Q	Stratham
Hobbs, Benj.	North Hampton(2)
Jacob	Rindge
James	Hampton
James	Rye
Jonathan	Rye
Joseph	Londonderry
Joseph	North Hampton
Morris	Hampton

Hobbs – Cont'd	
Morris	North Hampton
Nathaniel	North Hampton
Samuel	Deerfield
Thomas	North Hampton
Hockley, James	Peterborough
Hodgdon, Alex'r	Rochester
Alex'r Jr.	Rochester
Benjamin	Portsmouth
Charles	Portsmouth
Edmund, n.	Nottingham
Israel	Kensington
Israel	Northwood
John	Newington
John Jr.	Newington
John, Q	Weare
Jonathan, n.	Rochester
Joseph	Nottingham
Peter	Kensington
Phinehas	Portsmouth
Wm.	Rochester
Hodgsdon,	
Benjamin	Newington
Hodgson, Thomas	Portsmouth
Hogg,	
Allexander	Deering
David, n.	Dunbarton
George	Dunbarton
James, n.	Dunbarton
James	Londonderry
John	Dunbarton
John (Mr.) n.	Hampstead
Joseph	Londonderry
Robat, n.	Dunbarton
Robert	Hampstead
Robert	New Boston
Sam'l	Peterborough
William	Amherst
Hoit; see also Hoyt;	
Benj.	Rochester
Benjamin, n.	Sanbornton
Daniel	Northwood
Eastman, n.	Hopkinton
Enoch	Rochester

Hoit - Cont'd		Holt - Cont'd	
Ezekiel	Gilmanton	Humphrey	Londonderry
Jabez	Chester	Isaac	Amherst
John	Loudon	Jeremiah	Wilton
Jonathan	Stratham	Joseph	Wilton
Joseph	Boscawen	Joseph Jr.	Wilton
Joseph	Deerfield	Nathan	Pembroke
Joseph	Sanbornton	Reuben	Amherst
Moses	Weare	Samuel	Temple
Oliver	Concord	Simeon	Wilton
Philip	Weare	Thomas Jr.	Epsom
Reuben	Salisbury	Timothy	Wilton
Samuel	Deerfield	William	Epsom
Stephen	Northwood	Holton,	
Holbrook, Hoolbroock,		Jonathan	Westmoreland
Abiah	Portsmouth	Homans, George	Portsmouth
Adin	Keene	Homes,	
Joseph	Portsmouth	Jeremiah	Portsmouth
Peter	Richmond	Wm.	Portsmouth
Holl, Joseph	Chester	Hood, Richard	Concord
Holland, Stephen	Londonderry	William	Londonderry
Holmes; see also Holms, Homes;		Hook, Abraham	Sandown
Ephram Jr.	Barrington	Daniel	Seabrook
Noah	Barrington	Ezekiel	Epping
Robert	Portsmouth	Humphry	Hawke
Stetson	Winchester	Jacob	Kingston
William	Winchester	Joseph	Seabrook
Holms, Abraham	Peterborough	Josiah	Brentwood
Ephram	Barrington	William	Seabrook
John	Dunbarton	Hooke, Moses	Sandown
John	Londonderry	Hooker, John	Portsmouth
John (Lieut.) n.	Londonderry	Hooper, Jacob	New Boston
Joshua	Barrington	John	Portsmouth
Robert	Londonderry	Hopkins, Allen	Windham
Thomas	Londonderry	Benj.	Amherst
William	Dunbarton	Benjamin Jr.	Amherst
Holt, Abial	Wilton	David	Windham
Amos	Wilton	Eben'r	Amherst
Benjamin	Pembroke	Jas.	Londonderry
Daniel	Wilton	James	Society Land
Ebenezer Jr.	Amherst	John	Londonderry
Fifeld	Wilton	Robt.	Londonderry
Fifield Jr.	Wilton	Hopkinson,	
Fry	Pembroke	Jonathan	Exeter

Horn, Eben'r	Rochester
James	Rochester
Moses	Rochester
Peter	Rochester
Horne, John	Wakefield
Horton, Thomas	Richmond
Hough, Daniel	Lebanon
Lemuel	Lebanon
Houghton, Elijah	Winchester
Israel	Keene
John	Keene
Nehemiah	Winchester
Houston, Alex'dr	Acworth
James	Bedford
John (Rev.) n.	Bedford
Joseph	Bedford
Sam'l	Peterborough
[?] Stephen	Barrington
Hovey, Daniel	Enfield
Joseph	Hopkinton
Josiah	Enfield
Simeon	Weare
Hovy, Samuel, n.	Weare
How, Abner	Westmoreland
Daniel	Temple
David	Hopkinton
Eliakim	Henniker
Isaac	Amherst
James	Croydon
James	Rochester
Jotham	Hopkinton
Otis	Henniker
Peter	Hopkinton
Samuel	Amherst
Samuel	Westmoreland
Thomas	Barrington
Howard,	
Benjamin	Saville
James	Barrington
Samuel	Temple
Howe, Daniel	Westmoreland
George	Portsmouth
Joel	Amherst
Mark	Epping

Howlett, Davis	Keene
Thomas	Henniker
Hoyt, Hoyet; see also Hoit;	
Abner	Canterbury
Abner	Weare
Benjamin	Chester
Daniel, n.	Stratham
Eliphelet	Hawke
Ezra	Hopkinton
George	Weare
Jacob	Hopkinton
John	Chester
John	Newington
Jonathan	Newington
Joseph	Sandwich
Joseph (Capt.) n.	Stratham
Moses Jr.	Weare
Peaslee	Kingston
Samuel	Hopkinton
Stephen	Hopkinton
Thomas	Canterbury
Thomas	Dunbarton
Hubbard,	
Benjamin	Candia
Joseph	Claremont
Lemuel	Claremont
Leverett	Portsmouth
Oliver	Chesterfield
Richard	Kingston
Richard Jr.	Kingston
Hubburd, Amos	Chesterfield
Ephr'm	Chesterfield
Nathan	Rindge
Huckens, John	Barnstead
Huckings, James	Gilmanton
Huckins,	
Benjamin	Gilmanton
Isaac	Barnstead
John	Barrington
Joseph	Gilmanton
Joseph Jr.	Gilmanton
Thomas Jr.	Lee
Hudson, Benjamin	Chesterfield
Elisha	Wilton

Huestis, Aristides	Alstead	Huntoon - Cont'd	
Huey, Henry	Nottingham West	John Jr.	Kingston
Hughes, Richard	Amherst	John	Unity
Hull, George	Portsmouth	Philbrick	Kingston
Israel	Salem	Philip	Unity
Joseph	Salem	Huntress,	
Joseph Jr.	Salem	Christopher	Conway
Richard	Lee	Enoch	Portsmouth
Humphrey, John	Londonderry	Jonathan	Portsmouth
William	Winchester	Joseph	Newington
Humphry, Homphry,		Huntris, William	Newington
James Jr.	Londonderry	Huntriss,	
William, n.	Londonderry	Christopher	Newington
Hunkins, Benja.	Sandown	Jam's	Conway
Hunt, Henery	Kingston	Nathan	Newington
Henry	Hampstead	Hurd; see also Heard;	
James, n.	Keene	Justus	Gilsum
Jonathan	Hopkinton	Nathan	Newport
Joseph	Sandown	Samuel	Newport
Moses	Kingston	Shubael	Gilsum
Nathan	Sandown	Uzel, s.	Lempster
Philip	Sanbornton	Huse, Isrel	Sandown
Samuel	Epping	Jonathan	Sandown
Thomas	Lee	Joseph	Weare
Zacheus	Sandown	Moses, n.	Henniker
Hunter, Daniel	Londonderry	Sargent	Epping
James, n.	New Boston	Thomas	Dunbarton
John	Londonderry (2)	Huston, Caleb	Rindge
John, n.	New Boston	Hutcherson,	
Robert	Londonderry	John	Nottingham
Huntington, John	Weare	Hutchin, Samuel	Rye
Samuel, n.	Weare	Hutchings,	
Timothy	South Hampton	Jeremiah	Lee
Huntinton,		Sam'l	Portsmouth
Timothy	South Hampton	Hutchins, Huchens, Huhings,	
Hunton, Daniel	Salisbury	Gordon	Concord
Joseph	Weare	Hezekiah	Hampstead
Nathanel	Unity	Isaac	Winchester
Samuel	Unity	John	Portsmouth
Huntoon,		Sam'l	Lee
Benjamin	Kingston	Thomas	Winchester
Benj.	Salisbury	Thomas Jr.	Winchester
Caleb	Unity	William	Westmoreland
Charles	Unity	Hutchinson, Abner	Amherst

Hutchinson - Cont'd	
Benj.	Amherst
Dudley	Gilmanton
Elisha	Amherst
Elisha	Gilmanton
George	Wilton
Jonathan	Gilmanton
Nathan	Amherst
Nathan Jr.	Amherst
Samuel	Wilton
Thomas	Rindge
William	Hillsborough
Huthison,	
Ebenezer	Amherst
Hyde, John	Lebanon
Levi	Lebanon
Ilsley, John	Boscawen
Ingalls, Edmund	Richmond
Eldad	Atkinson
Henry	Richmond
John	Atkinson
Jon'a	Rindge
Josiah	Rindge
Nath'l	Rindge
Nath'l	Sandown
Samuel	Sandown
Simeon	Rindge
Ives, Joseph	Claremont
Jack, Andrew, n.	New Boston
Jackman, Jakman,	
Benjamin	Boscawen
George	Boscawen
George Jr.	Boscawen
John	Boscawen
Moses	Boscawen
Richard	Conway
Samuel	Boscawen
Simeon	Boscawen
Jacks; see also Jaques;	
Sam'l	Chester
Jackson,	
Benjamin	Nottingham
Bennan	Lee
Caleb	Rochester

Jackson - Cont'd	
Clem't	Portsmouth
Daniel	Portsmouth
Daniel Jr.	Portsmouth
Eben	Barrington
George	Portsmouth
Hall	Portsmouth
James	Rochester
Jno.	Portsmouth
Joseph	Nottingham
Joseph	Portsmouth
Nath'll Sr.	Portsmouth
Nathaniel Jr.	Portsmouth
Richard	Portsmouth
Robert	Newmarket
Samuel	Lee
Sam'll	Portsmouth
Jacobs, Daniel	Barnstead
Jaffrey,	
George, n.	Portsmouth
James,	
Benjamin	Gilmanton
Benjamin	Kensington
Benjamin Jr.	Kensington
David	Kensington
Edmund	Sandown
Frances	Epping
Francis	Northwood
Israel	Kensington
John	Kensington
Jonathan	Gilmanton
Joshua	Hampton
Kinsley H.	Exeter
Jameson,	
James	Windham
John	Dunbarton
Thomas	Windham
Will'm	Windham
Janvrin,	
Ebenezer	Portsmouth
Geo.	Portsmouth
Jaques; see also Jacks;	
John	Londonderry
Jeffry, John	Gilmanton

Jemeson,	
Alexander	Society Land
Hugh	Dunbarton
Jemson, John	Salisbury
Jenison, Lot	Hillsborough
Jenkes, Moses	Brentwood
Jenkins,	
Cornelius	Rochester
Stephen	Rochester
William, n.	Lee
William Jr., n.	Lee
William	Portsmouth
Jenks, Jeremiah	Newport
Jennes, Job	Rye
Job Jr.	Rye
John	Rye
Joshua	Hampton
Joshua Jr.	Hampton
Nathaniel	Rye
Richard	Rye
Rich'd III	Rye
Sam'l	Pembroke
Jenness,	
Francis	Rye
Frances Jr.	Rye
Isaac	North Hampton
John	Rye
Jon'a	Rye
Joseph, s.	Rye
Richard	Deerfield
Rich'd Jr.	Rye
Sam'l	Rye
Sam'l Jr.	Rye
Thos.	Deerfield
Thomas	Hampton
Jennis, Aaron	Rochester
Daniel, n.	Rochester
David	Rochester
John	Rochester
Moses	Rochester
Paul	Rochester
Wm	Rochester
Wm Jr.	Rochester
Jewell; see also Juell.	

Jewell, Asahel	Winchester
Daniel	Stratham
David	Stratham
Jacob, n.	Sandwich
Jacob	Stratham
John	Weare
John Jr., n.	Weare
Joseph	Brentwood
Mark, n.	Sandwich
Jewet, Ezekiel	Temple
Stephen	Rindge
Jewett, Andrew	Sanbornton
Benjamin	Hopkinton
David	Candia
David	Deerfield
Edward	Rindge
Ezekiel	Rindge
James, n.	Hopkinton
John	Hopkinton
John Jr.	Hopkinton
Jonathan, n.	Stratham
Mark	Hopkinton
Moses	Hopkinton
Samuel	Hopkinton
Jiles, Joseph	Rochester
Jillson, Jonathan	Richmond
Johnson; see also Jonson;	
Abner	Chesterfield
Benj.	Canterbury
Benj.	Epping
Benjamin Jr.	Epping
Benj.	Northwood
Caleb	Chesterfield
Caleb, n.	Hampstead
Charles	Chesterfield
Cornelius	Concord
Daniel	Westmoreland
David	Westmoreland
Ebenezer	Salisbury
Edmund, Q	Weare
Elisha	Hampton
Enoch, Q	Weare
Ezra	Wilton
Ichabod	Allenstown

Johnson - Cont'd		Jones - Cont'd	
Israel	Chesterfield	Ephraim	Weare
Ithamar	Dublin	Evan	Salem
James	Epping	Ezra	Claremont
James	Hampton	Ezra	Hawke
Jeremiah	Kingston	George	Lee
Jesse, n.	Hampstead	Jacob	South Hampton
John	Atkinson	James	Lebanon
John	Hampton	James	Portsmouth (2)
John	Salem	Jehu	Canaan
John	Sanbornton	John, n.	Hopkinton
Joseph	Brentwood	John	Lee
Joseph	Hampton	Jonthen	Hawke
Lemul	Brentwood	Joseph	Deerfield
Moses	Dublin	Joseph	Lee
Moses	Northwood	Joseph	Rochester
Moses	Nottingham West	Joseph	South Hampton
Nathaniel	Hampton	Joseph Jr.	South Hampton
Obadiah, Q	Kensington	Joshua	Portsmouth
Peter	Rye	Josiah	Londonderry
Samuel	Hampstead	Levi	Leavitt's Town
Samuel Jr.	Hampstead	Matthias	Lee
Sam'l	Northwood	Moses, n.	Hopkinton
Samuel	Salem	Nathan	Amherst
Simeon	Dublin	Nathan Jr.	Amherst
Simon	Epping	Nathan	Hawke
Simon	Rye	Nathan Jr.	Hawke
Simon	Salem	Samuel	Canaan
Stephen	Hampstead	Samuel	Chester
Stephen	Londonderry	Sam'l	Hillsborough
Timothy	Salem	Samuel	Rochester
Willis	Westmoreland	Simon, n.	Hinsdale
Zebadiah	Temple	Thomas (Ens.)	Claremont
Johnston,		Timothy	Epping
Benjamin	Epsom	William	Hillsborough
Ser Wm.	Londonderry	William Jr.	Hillsborough
Jones, Alexander	Portsmouth	William	Newcastle
Asa	Claremont	Jonson,	
Benj.	Lee	Benjamin Jr.	Northwood
Benjamin	Lee	Jordon, Peter	Loudon
Daniel Esq., n.	Hinsdale	Joslen, Richard	Canaan
Daniel	South Hampton	Samuel	Canaan
E. Jr.	Lee	Joslyn, James	Henniker
Ebenezer	Lee	Nath'l	Henniker

Joy, Joseph	Newmarket
Judd,	
Ebenezer, n.	Claremont
Ebenezer Jr., n.	Claremont
Enoch, n.	Claremont
Judkins,	
Benjamin	Deerfield
Benjamin	Kingston
Caleb	Kingston
Henry	Kingston
Job	Brentwood
Job	Meredith
John	Kingston
John Jr.	Kingston
Jonathan	Deerfield
Joseph	Deerfield
Joseph	Hopkinton
Joseph	Kingston
Josiah	Hopkinton
Leonard	Salisbury
Robert	Epping
Samuel	Sandown
Sam'l, n.	Unity
Juell; see also Jewell;	
Henery	South Hampton
Kain, Barnbass	Bedford
Kalley, Hugh	Londonderry
Peter	Londonderry
Kanear, John	Newcastle
Karr, John	Chester
John	Londonderry (2)
Sam'l	Londonderry
Thos.	New Boston
Keef, Michael	Amherst
Keep, Lenord, n.	Westmoreland
Keing, Jab., n.	Chesterfield
Kelcey; see also Kelse, Kelsey;	
Absalom	Newport
Giels	Newport
Jesse	Newport
Lemer	Newport
Kelcy, Roswel	Newport
Kelley, James	Stratham
John (Deac'n) n.	Salem

Kelley – Cont'd	
Philip	Epping
Sam'l	Pembroke
Kellom, see Killom.	
Kelly, Daniel	Sandown
Darby	Brentwood
David	Kingston
Edward	Sanbornton
Jacob	Gilmanton
John	Atkinson
Rich'd	Salem
Samuel	Dunbarton
Samuel	Hampstead
Samuel	Salem
Kelse; see also Kelcey, Kelsey;	
James	Nottingham
Kelsey,	
Alexander	Londonderry
Kelso,	
Alexander, n.	New Boston
Daniel, n.	New Boston
Jonathan	Londonderry
William, n.	New Boston
Kemp, Ezekiel	Winchester
Kempton, Stephen	Richmond
Kendal, Reuben	Westmoreland
Kendall,	
John Jr.	Amherst
Nathan	Amherst
Kendrick, Kindrick,	
Benj.	Amherst
Benj.	Deerfield
David	Deerfield
Kenear; see also Kanear;	
John	Nottingham
Kennedy, William	Bedford
Kenney, Daniel	Wilton
David	Wilton
Kennison,	
Bickford	Stratham
Kennisson,	
Peter	Portsmouth
Kenniston,	
Henry	Stratham

Kenson, Thomas	Newmarket	Kimball - Cont'd	
Kenston,		John	Wakefield
Franses	Nottingham	Joseph	Hampstead
Kent, Job	Hampstead	J seph Esq., n.	Henniker
John	Hampstead	Joseph	Weare
Keyes, Ephraim	Acworth	Joshua, n.	Henniker
Simon	Wilton	Joshua	Pembroke
William	Acworth	Mikel	Pembroke
Keys, Daniel	Westmoreland	Moses	Amherst
Edward	Acworth	Moses.	Hampstead
John	Wilton	Moses	Hopkinton
Kezar, Reuben	Canterbury	Nathan	Hopkinton
Kidder, Benjamin	Londonderry	Nathanael	Gilmanton
Josiah	Amherst	Nathaniell	Hopkinton
Nathaniel	Lebanon	Noah	Wakefield
Samson	Londonderry	Oliver	Salem
Samuel	Alstead	Oliver Jr.	Salem
Thomas	Alstead	Peter	Boscawen
Kiellie, Ebenezer	Barrington	Philip	Concord
Kilbarn,		Phinehas	Concord
Ebenezer	Gilsum	Porter	Brentwood
Kilborn, John	Claremont	Reuben	Concord
Kilbourn, Joel	Gilsum	Richard	Rindge
Kilburn, Josiah	Gilsum	Richard Jr.	Rindge
Josiah Jr.	Gilsum	Richard	Salem
Killey, Jonathan	Epping	Robert	Exeter
Killom,		Samuel	Hopkinton
Ebenezer, n.	Winchester	Samuel	Pembroke
Killy, Joseph (Capt.), n.,		Stephen	Concord
	Nottingham West	Thomas	Weare
Kimball, Aaron	Hopkinton	Timothy	Concord
Abel	Hopkinton	William, n.	Henniker
Abraham	Hopkinton	William	Pembroke
Asa	Concord	Kimbel, John	Meredith
Barnard	Salem	Kimbell,	
Benjamin	Exeter	Benj. (Dec'n) n.	Hampstead
Daniel	Rochester	Ebenezer, n.	Hampstead
David	Pembroke	Joseph Jr., n.	Hampstead
Dudley	Brentwood	Ruben	Hopkinton
Eben'r	Canterbury	Kimboll, Sam'l (Coro'l), n.,	
Ezekiel	Weare		Henniker
Henry	Amherst	Kindrick, see Kendrick.	
James	Hopkinton	King; see also Keing;	
John	Concord	George	Portsmouth

King - Cont'd	
George Jr.	Portsmouth
Richard	Wilton
Silas	Alstead
Thomas	Conway
Zebulun	Deerfield
Kingman, John	Barrington
Kingsbery, Abijah	Chesterfield
Kingsbury,	
Absalom	Alstead
Daniel	Keene
Nathaniel	Keene
Kingsley, James	Richmond
Kinisen; see also	Kennesson,
Kinneson, Kinsen, Kinson;	
Daniel	Chesterfield
Kinison,	
Solomon	Gilmanton
Kiniston,	
Jonathan	Epping
Kinkead, John	Londonderry
John	Salem
Kinnem[?], Ben	Wakefield
Kinneson; see also	Kennisson,
Kinisen, Kinsen, Kinson;	
John	Lee
Kinney, Amos	Nottingham West
Kinnison,	
Jonathan, n.	Newmarket
Joseph	Deerfield
Lewis	Newmarket
Kinnisone,	
Josiah	Lee
Kinsen, Samuel	Allenstown
Kinsman, Aaron	Bow
Kinson,	
Valentine	Northwood
Kinstone, Aron	Newmarket
Kitson, Richard	Portsmouth
Kittredge,	
Solomon	Amherst
Knap, Abiel	Richmond
Knight, Abraham	Nottingham
Charles	Rochester

Knight - Cont'd	
Eliphalet	Salem
Enoch	Atkinson
John	Atkinson
John Jr.	Atkinson
John 3d	Atkinson
Joseph	Atkinson
Joseph Jr.	Atkinson
Joseph	Rochester
Joshua	Atkinson
Joshua, n.	Rochester
Temple	Portsmouth
Tristram	Atkinson
Wm.	Portsmouth
Wm.	Rochester
Knights, Amaziah	Claremont
Knolton, see Knowlton.	
Knowels, Ezekiel	Candia
Knowles, Amos	Candia
Amos	Hampton
Amos Jr.	Hampton
David	North Hampton
David	Northwood
James	Rochester
Jeremiah	Hampton
John	Chester
John Jr.	Chester
John	Rochester
Jonathan	Epsom
Jonathan	North Hampton
Joseph	Chester
Joseph	North Hampton
Josiah	Epsom
Nathan	Chester
Samuel	Rye
Samuel Jr.	Rye
Simon	Epsom
Knowls, Nathaniel	Sandwich
Knowlton, Knolton,	
David	Epsom
John	Boscawen
John	Dublin
Jonathan	Northwood
Thomas	Northwood

Knox, David	Allenstown	Lake - Cont'd	
James	Pembroke	George	Rindge
John	Pembroke	Thomas	Newcastle
John Jr.	Pembroke	Lakeman, Lakman,	
Timothy	Pembroke	Nathanel	Pembroke
William	Allenstown	Nathaniel Jr.	Pembroke
William	Conway	Samuel	Pembroke
Will'm	Pembroke	Lamas, Samuel, n.	Lee
Kyel, John	Windham	Lamb, Josiah	Chesterfield
Lad, Benjamin	Kingston	Lampere, Simon	North Hampton
John	Kingston	Lampery, Samuel	Kensington
John	Pembroke	Lampre, Henery	Kensington
John	Unity	Lamprey,	
Nathaniel	Unity	Benjamin	North Hampton
Paul	Epping	Daniel	Hampton
Timothy, n.	Hinsdale	John	Hampton
Ladd, Benj., n.	Deerfield	John Jr.	Hampton
Daniel	Deerfield	John	North Hampton
Daniel	Loudon	Moris	North Hampton
Daniel	Salem	Nathaniel	Hampton
Dudley	Deerfield	Reuben	Hampton
Edward	Exeter	Lampson,	
Elias	Sandwich	Jonathan	Amherst
Elias Jr.	Sandwich	Lamson, Joseph	Exeter
Eliphalet	Windham	Samuel	Exeter
Isaac	Sandown	William	Amherst
James, n.	Unity	Lancaster, see Lankester.	
Jeremiah	Canterbury	Lane, Lain; see also Layn;	
John	Sandwich	Ebenezer	Hampton
Nathaniel, n.	Epping	Jesse	Newport
Paul Jr.	Epping	John	Candia
Samuel	Gilmanton	John	Chester
Simeon	Nottingham	John Jr.	Chester
Tim'o	Windham	John	Hampton
Timothy Jr.	Windham	John	Kensington
Laighen, John	Barrington	John	Newport
Laighton; see also Leighton;		John	Sanbornton
David	Rochester	Joshua	Stratham
George	Newington	Josiah	Hampton
Isaac	Barrington	Oliver Wellington	Hampton
Joel	Newington	Robert	Newport
Paul	Portsmouth	Sam'l Jr.	Stratham
Lain, see Lane.		Samuel	Stratham
Lake, Daniel	Rindge	Simon	Hampton

Lane - Cont'd
Ward	Hampton
William	Hampton
William Jr.	Hampton
Lang, Bickford	Rye
Daniel	Portsmouth
Henry	Portsmouth
John	Portsmouth (2)
Mark	Portsmouth
Nath'l	Portsmouth
Samuel	Portsmouth
William	Saville
Langdell, Joseph	Amherst
Livermore	New Boston
Langdon, John	Portsmouth (2)
Joseph	Portsmouth
Ric'd	Portsmouth
Sam	Portsmouth
Sam'l Jr.	Portsmouth
William	Portsmouth
Langley,	
Eldad, n.	Nottingham
Jonathan	Nottingham
Samuel	Lee
Langly, James	Deerfield
Thomas Jr.	Lee
Langmade,	
Samiel	Newcastle
Langmaid, Henry	Newcastle
Samuel	Lee
Lankeest, Henry	Salem
Lankester, Moses	Londonderry
Lankster, John	Salem
Larkin, Patrick	Bedford
Larrabe, Stephen	Keene
Larrance,	
Daniel, n.	Monadnock
Lary, Dan'l	Sanbornton
Lasell, John	Enfield
Laskey,	
William, s.	Lee
Latham, Arthur	Winchester
James	Winchester
Joseph	Winchester

Lathrop, Samuel	Canaan
Sluman	Lebanon
Laury; see also Lary;	
Stephen	Newcastle
Lavrien, Benjamin	Kingston
Law, Andrew	Temple
Lawrance; see also Larrance;	
David Jr.	Epping
David	Londonderry
Gordan	Meredith
Nathnel	Winchester
Nathaniel T'is [i.e., 3rd],	
	Winchester
Lawrans,	
Edward	Epping
Lawrence,	
David	Epping
Micah (Rev.), n.,	
	Winchester
Layn, John	Lee
Leach; see also Leech, Litch;	
Azariah	Westmoreland
Isaac	Westmoreland
Jacob	Westmoreland
Joseph	Portsmouth
Josiah	Portsmouth
Josiah	Westmoreland
Josiah Jr.	Westmoreland
Seth	Westmoreland
Sherebiah	Westmoreland
Zephaniah	Westmoreland
Lear, Leear,	
Benj.	Portsmouth
Elexandr	Rye
Georg Walker	Saville
John	Newcastle
Joseph	Saville
Nathaniel	Portsmouth
Sam'l	Portsmouth
Tobias	Portsmouth
Learned,	
Benjamin	Dublin
Ezekiel	Rindge
Leat, Asa, n.	Claremont

Leat - Cont'd	
Benj., n.	Claremont
Leathers,	
Abednego	Nottingham
Abiel	Nottingham
Edward	Lee
John	Lee
Nicholas	Nottingham
Vowel	Nottingham
Leavit, Joseph	Wakefield
Leavitt; see also Levatt, Levitt;	
Benjamin	North Hampton
Benjamin	Seabrook
Benjmin	Stratham
Carr	Leavitt's Town
Daniel	Brentwood (2)
John	Leavitt's Town
John	North Hampton
John	Stratham
Jonathan	Hampton
Jonathan	Stratham
Joshua	Deerfield
Josiah	Stratham
Moses	North Hampton
Sam	Stratham
Simon	Leavitt's Town
Thomas	Brentwood
Thomas	Deerfield
Thomas	Hampton
Thomas	North Hampton
Lebbee, Arther	Rye
Beneet	Epsom
Isaac	Epsom
LeBourveau, John	Keene
Leech; see also Leach, Litch;	
Joseph, n.	Salem
William, n.	Salem
Leigh, Joseph	Portsmouth
Thomas	Portsmouth
Leighton; see also Laighton;	
Giddon	Barrington
James	Barrington
Leland, Eleazer	Croydon
Jacob	Croydon
Lennon, Thomas	Londonderry
Leonard, John	Allenstown
Epharim	Westmoreland
Letch, William	Wilton
Levatt, Samuel	Deerfield
Levitt, Gedion	Sanbornton
Jonathan Jr.	Stratham
Leweis, John	Portsmouth
Lewes, James	Monadnock
Joseph	Henniker
Lewis, Gideon	Claremont
John Jr.	Portsmouth
Seth	Claremont
Thomas	Dublin
Thomas	Wilton
Lews, Samuel	Claremont
Libbee; see also Lebbee;	
Abraham	Rye
Libbey, George	Portsmouth
Ham	Nottingham
Isaac	Rochester
Jeremiah	Portsmouth
Paul	Rochester
Lien, James	Bedford
Lifford, Liford, see Lyford.	
Linn, Joseph	Chester
Litch, James	Londonderry
Little, Abner	Hampstead
Benj. Jr.	Hampstead
Bond	Deering
Daniel	Hampstead
Daniel Jr.	Hampstead
Enoch	Boscawen
Friend	Boscawen
Henry	Salem
James	Atkinson
James	Bedford
Joseph	Atkinson
John	Bedford
Moses	Hampstead
Samuel	Atkinson
Samuel	Hampstead
Stephen, n.	Portsmouth
Taylor	New Boston

Little - Cont'd	
Thomas	Atkinson
Tristram	Hampstead
Livermore,	
Jonathan	Wilton
Livingston, John	Londonderry
John, n.	New Boston
Robert	New Boston
Wm. (Lieut.)	New Boston
Lock, David	Rye
Edward, n.	Gilmanton
Edward	Kensington
Edw'd	Rochester
Elijah	Rye (2)
Ephraim	Epsom
Francis	Epsom
James	Rye
Jeremiah	Rye
Jethro	Barrington
John Jr.	Rye
Jonathan	Hampton
Jonathan	Rye
Joseph	Rye
Joseph Jr.	Rye
Joshua	Rye
Richard	Rye
Richard III	Rye
Samuel	Brentwood
Samuel	Hampton
Simon	Barrington
Timothy Blake	Kensington
William	Barrington
William Jr.	Barrington
William	Chester
Locke,	
Ebenezer	Rindge
Moses	Epsom
Lomprey, Morris	Northwood
Long, Ebenezer	Kingston
Joseph	Chester
Pierse	Portsmouth
Robt.	South Hampton
Stephen	Sandown
Longfellow, Jacob	Deerfield

Looge; see also Louge, Lougee;	
Jesse	Gilmanton
Lord, John	Portsmouth
Robert	Exeter
William	Barnstead
Lorde, Nath'l, n.	Newmarket
Louge; see also Looge, Lougee;	
Nehemiah	Gilmanton
Lougee, Gilman	Gilmanton
Gilman Jr.	Gilmanton
Love, William	Hillsborough
Lovejoy, Abiel	Conway
Benjamin	Hillsborough
Caleb	Pembroke
Caleb Jr.	Pembroke
Chandler	Concord
Chandler	Pembroke
David	Pembroke
Francis	Amherst
Henry	Concord
Henry	Wilton
Hezekiah	Amherst
Jacob	Amherst
John	Amherst
John	Rindge
John Jr.	Rindge
Samuel	Wilton
Loveren,	
Ebenezer	Kensington
Lovering,	
Benjamin	Rindge
Eben	North Hampton
Eben'r	North Hampton
John	North Hampton
Simon D.	North Hampton
Lovet, John	Salem
Low, Jacob, n.	Stratham
Joseph	Portsmouth
William	Amherst
Lowd, Edward	Portsmouth
Joseph	Portsmouth
Lowel, David	Epping
John Jr.	Salem
Stephen Jr.	Nottingham West

Lowell, James	Hawke		McAllester,	
Moses	Raby		Ananias	Amherst
Reuben	Kingston		Archibald	New Boston
Loynds, Charls	Claremont		Daniel, n.	New Boston
David Jr.	Claremont		Isaac	Monadnock
Lucy, Alexander	Nottingham		James	Bedford
John	Deerfield		John, n.	New Boston
Ludy[?], John	Stratham		McAllster,	
Lufken, Stephen	Chester		Richard	Bedford
Lull, Simon	Deerfield		McBreney,	
Lumper, Levi	Leavitt's Town		William	Saville
Lund, Jonathan	Amherst		McBrid, John	Monadnock
Lunt, Daniel	Portsmouth		McBride, Hugh	Portsmouth
John	Epping		McCalaster,	
Lyerd, Thomes	Exeter		Archebald	Londonderry
Lyford, Liford,			McCalley,	
Biley	Brentwood		James	Dunbarton
James Gilman	Loudon		John	Hillsborough
John	Canterbury		McCay,	
John	Epping		Alexander	Windham
Moses	Brentwood		John	Windham
Stephen, n.	Newmarket		Thomas	Windham
Thomas	Exeter		McClary, John Jr.	Epsom
Lyman, Elias	Lebanon		McCleary; see also McClerey;	
John	Enfield		David	Londonderry
Lynch, Morish	Society Land		John	Society Land
Lynd, David	Claremont		Thom	Londonderry
Lyon, Aaron	Alstead		Thomas	Londonderry
John	Deering		William	Bedford
Jonathan	Amherst		McClellan, Hugh	Candia
Josiah	Alstead		Joseph	Chester
Lyons, James	Londonderry		McClenche,	
McAdam, Samuel	Windham		John	Londonderry
McAdams, John	Londonderry		McClerey; see also McCleary;	
Robert	Londonderry		David	Bedford
Samuel	Londonderry		McClery, John	Epsom
William	Londonderry		McClintok,	
McAffe,			Alexander	Hillsborough
Mansfield	Chester		John	Hillsborough
McAfee; see also McKafee;			Nicheall	Derryfield
Hugh	Chester		William	Derryfield
McAlester, John	Londonderry		McCluer, James	Acworth
Samuel	Peterborough		Jonathan	Deerfield
McAllaster, George	Londonderry		Samuel	Deerfield

McClur, Robert   Londonderry
McClurg, John   Londonderry
McCollam, Alexd'r   Londonderry
McColom, Robert   Londonderry
   Thomas   New Boston
McConiel, John   Piermont
McConnel, Sam'l (Capt.), n.,
     Pembroke
McConnell, Moses   Pembroke
   Thomas   Nottingham
McCordey,
   John, n.   Dunbarton
McCoy, Charls   Allenstown
   Charls   Nottingham
   William   Peterborough
McCreles, John   Epsom
   William   Epsom
McCrelles, Henry   Epsom
McCrilles, David   Canterbury
   James   Meredith
   John   Deerfield
   John   Nottingham
McCurdy, John   Surry
   Samuel   Surry
McCuthen, Phedris   Pembroke
McDaniel,
   Jeremiah   Canterbury
   John   Canterbury
   John   Pembroke
   Nehemiah   Pembroke
   Robert   Pembroke
   William Jr.   Barrington
McDaniels,
   William   Barrington
McDonell, Randel   Raby
McDowell,
   Alexander   Winchester
McDuffee, Daniel   Londonderry
   James   Rochester
   John   Londonderry
   Matthew   Bedford
   Wm   Rochester
McElroy, James   Chesterfield
McFarland, Robert   Londonderry

McFarlend, John   Wilton
McFerson,
   James, n.   New Boston
   James Jr., n.   New Boston
   Rowl, n.   New Boston
   Samuel   Chester
McGaffey, Andrew   Epsom
   John   Epsom
   Neal   Epsom
McGaw, Robert   New Boston
McGinis,
   Barnabas   New Boston
McGregore, D.   Londonderry
   James   Londonderry (2)
McIlvaine, Rob't   Windham
McIlvane, Dan'l   Windham
McInter, James   Portsmouth
McIntosh,
   Alex'r, s.   Raby
   James   Raby
   John   Bedford
   John   Londonderry
   John, n.   New Boston
McIntyer, N.   Portsmouth
McKafee, Archibald   Chester
McKeen, MacKeen,
   David   Londonderry
   James   Amherst
   John   Londonderry
   Robert   Londonderry
   William   Deering
   William   Peterborough
McKinley, Robert   Chester
McKinney, John   Bedford
McKnight, see McNight.
McLaughlin, MacLaughlin,
   John   Bedford
   John, n.   New Boston
   John Jr., n.   New Boston
   Thos   Bedford
McLaughton, see Macglaton.
McLucas, Danieal   Pembroke
McMahon, Mackmahawn,
   John   Portsmouth

Mc Masten,	
Wiallem	Chester
Mc Master,	
Thomas	Chester
Mc Miclel, Patrick	Chesterfield
Mc Millan, And'w	Conway
Arch'd	New Boston
Daniel	New Boston
John, n.	New Boston
John Jr.	New Boston
Mc Murphey, John	Peterborough
Mc Murphy, Mac Murphy,	
Alex'r	Derryfield
Archibald	Londonderry
George	Londonderry
James	Londonderry
Robert	Londonderry
Robt. Jr.	Londonderry
McNeal, Wm	Rochester
McNeall, Daniel	Hillsborough
McNee, William	Peterborough
William Jr.	Peterborough
McNeill, Daniel	Londonderry
Josiah	New Boston
Robt.	Londonderry
McNiele,	
William, n.	New Boston
McNiell, Daniel, n.	New Boston
William	New Boston
McNight, James	Derryfield
McPherson, see Mc Ferson.	
McQuaid, Jacob	Bedford
Macclure, David	Portsmouth
Mace, Andrew	Hampton
Sam'l	North Hampton
Macglaton, Thomas	Salem
Mack, Andrew	Londonderry
Archibald	Londonderry
Dan'l	Peterborough
Elisha	Gilsum
Joseph	Alstead
Joseph	Londonderry
Nathan	Alstead
Mackey, Benj.	Portsmouth

Macordy, Robert	Londonderry
Magoon, Joseph	Loudon
Moses, n.	Brentwood
Thomas	Loudon
Magrath, Roger	Hampstead
Main, Josiah	Rochester
Maleham, Joseph	Wakefield
Man, Abraham	Richmond
Ase	Richmond
Gideon	Richmond
Hezekiah	Keene
Janes	Pembroke
John	Pembroke
John (Dea'n), n.	Pembroke
Nehemiah	Westmoreland
Peter	Portsmouth
Samuel	Pembroke
William	Pembroke
Mann, Theodore	Monadnock
Manning, Thomas	Portsmouth
Manser, William	Temple
Mansfield,	
Achilles	Keene
Elijah	Temple
George	Londonderry
James	Chesterfield
Levi	Rindge
Manson, Josiah	Barrington
Manuaell, Antony	Bow
Manuel, John	Boscawen
Moses	Boscawen
Marbel, Joseph	Winchester
Marble, Calab	Salem
March, Clement	Portsmouth
George (Capt.) n.	Stratham
John	Londonderry
Joseph	Deerfield
Samuel	Hawke
Stephen, n.	Hampstead
Mardeen,	
Nathaniel Jr.	Rye
Marden, Ben	Rye
Benjamen	Rye
Benjamin III	Rye

Marden - Cont'd		Marshel - Cont'd	
Hinkson	Barrington	William (Capt.) n., Hampstead	
Israel	Portsmouth	Marstes, John (Doct'r), n.,	
James	Barrington		Newmarket
James	Epsom	Marston,	
James	Portsmouth	Benjamin Jr.	North Hampton
John	Epping	Caleb	North Hampton
John	Portsmouth	Daniel, n.	Deerfield
Joseph	Rye	David	North Hampton
Nathan	Epsom	Elisha	Hampton
Nathaniel	Rye	Ephraim	Hampton
Stephen	Chester	Isaac, n.	Newmarket
Thos.	Portsmouth	Isaac	North Hampton
William	Rye	James	Brentwood
Mardon, Samuel	Rye	Jeremiah (Capt.), n.,	
Marill, John	Dunbarton		Hampton
Mariner, Meriner,		Jere'h Jr.	Hampton
John	Stratham	John	Hampton
Nicholas, n.	Stratham	John	Leavitt's Town
Marison, see Morrison.		John, n.	Newmarket
Markham, William Acworth		John	North Hampton
Marks, John	Gilsum	Jonathan	Hampton
Marsh; see also Mash;		Jonathan Jr.	Hampton
John	Londonderry	Joseph	Salisbury
Samuel	Londonderry	Nathaniel	Salisbury
Samuel	Nottingham West	Philip	Hampton
Thomas	Nottingham West	Reuben	Leavitt's Town
Marshal, Philip	Londonderry	Reuben	Meredith
Marshall, Aaron	Temple	Reuben Jr.	Meredith
Benj.	Nottingham West	Samuel	Brentwood
Daniel	Londonderry	Samuel	Hampton
David	Packersfield	Simon	Deerfield
George	Portsmouth	Simon	Hampton
Geo. Jr.	Portsmouth	Simeon	North Hampton
Hawly	Brentwood	Thomas	North Hampton
John	Londonderry	Winroup	Brentwood
John Sr.	Portsmouth	Martain,	
John Jr.	Portsmouth	Jonathan	Weare
Obdeir	Portsmouth	Reuben	Weare
Richard	Londonderry	Martin, Elezer	Richmond
Richard	Nottingham West	George	Richmond
Thomas	Temple	Henry	Concord
William	Portsmouth	James	Bedford
Marshel, Moses, n., Deerfield		James	Pembroke

Martin - Cont'd		Matlon, John	Deerfield
John	Richmond	Matthews, Abner	Claremont
John Jr.	Richmond	Abner Jr.	Claremont
Jon'a.	Wilton	Joel	Claremont
Joseph	Lebanon	Thomas	Bedford
Moses	Richmond	Maxfield, Joshua	Weare
Peter	Richmond	Nathaniel	Candia
Robert	Newcastle	Eliphelet	Sandwich
Th'o.	Portsmouth	Maynard, Caleb	Temple
William	Pembroke	Meacham, Samuel	Enfield
William Jr.	Pembroke	Mead, Benjamin	Meredith
William	Portsmouth	Benj.	Newmarket
Marvin, Giles	Alstead	John	Deerfield
John	Surry	John	Hillsborough
Mash, Henery	Gilmanton	John	Meredith
John	Gilmanton	John	Newmarket
Moses	Keene	Thomas	Portsmouth
Mason, Benj.	Dublin	William	Meredith
Benjamin	Hampton	Meader,	
Benj.	North Hampton	Elijah, n.	Stratham
Daniel	Stratham	Joseph, n.	Lee
Edmund	Hampton	Marke	Lee
Edward	Stratham	Nicolas	Lee
Francis	Stratham	Means, Robert	Amherst
James	Deerfield	Medcalf, Burges	Piermont
John	Newmarket	Michaell	Chesterfield
Joseph	Epping	Meeder, Meder,	
Joseph	Packersfield	Benj., Q	Rochester
Joseph, n.	Stratham	John	Newmarket
Joseph Jr.	Stratham	Jon'a, Q	Rochester
Josiah	Hampton	Joseph, Q	Rochester
Oliver	Richmond	Nath'l, Q	Rochester
Robert	Deerfield	Meeds, Stephen	Portsmouth
Massey, Daniel	Salem	Melcher,	
George	Portsmouth	Benjamin	Kensington
Jonathan	Salem	Edward	Kensington
Massuerre,		James	Portsmouth
Francis	Portsmouth	John	Kensington
Mathes, Matthes; see also Methes;		John	Portsmouth (2)
Gashom	Loudon	Nath'l	Portsmouth
Gideon	Lee	Melchir, John	Gilmanton
James	Bedford	Mellondy,	
Robert	Bedford	Wm. Jr.	Amherst
Samuel	Lee	Mells, John	Barrington

Meloon,	
Abraham, n.	Weare
Jonathan	Epping
Joseph	Newmarket
Nath'l (Lieut.) n.	Deerfield
Nathaniel	Salisbury
Nathaniel Jr.	Salisbury
Samuel	Newmarket
Melvein,	
Benjamain	Chester
Melven,	
Benjamin, n.	Winchester
Benjamin Jr., n.	Winchester
Mendum, John	Lee
Nathaniel	Portsmouth
Merill, Benjamin	Amherst
David	Derryfield
James	Stratham
John	Salem
John Jr.	Salem
Meritt, Ebenezer	Newport
Merrell, James	Atkinson
Merrick, Merick,	
Netheniel, n.	Henniker
Merriell, Daniel	Meredith
Merril, Abel	Nottingham West
Abel Jr.	Atkinson
Aseph, n.	Deerfield
Benj., n.	Hopkinton
Caleb	Boscawen
Isaac	Nottingham West
John	Deerfield
John	Nottingham West
Joseph, n.	Deerfield
Joseph, n.	Salem
Nath'l	Nottingham West
Natha'el	Nottingham West
Nathel Ters [3rd]	" "
Peter, n.	Salem
William	Nottingham West
Merrill; see also Marill, Merill,	
Merrell, Merriell, Merril;	
Abel	Atkinson
Abiathar	Seabrook

Merrill - Cont'd	
Abraham	Derryfield (2)
Amos	Chester
Amos	Conway
Amos, n.	Windham
Benjamin	Stratham
Daniel	Salem
David	Salem
Dean	Pembroke
Eliphe	Seabrook
Eliphelet	South Hampton
Eliphelet Jr.	South Hampton
Enoch, n.	Stratham
Enoch Jr., n.	Stratham
Ezekiel	East Kingston
Ford	Stratham
Hallawill	Chesterfield
Jesse	Salem
John	Atkinson
Jonathan	Concord
Jonathan	Derryfield
Joseph	South Hampton
Joseph	Stratham
Moses	Derryfield
Nath'l	Salem
Nehemiah	Chesterfield
Parley	Salem
Peter	Windham
Peter Jr.	Windham
Richard	Hopkinton
Robart	Deerfield
Stephen	Chester
Thos.	Conway
Thos. Jr.	Conway
Thomas	Kingston
Timothy	Salem
William	Conway
Merritt, see Meritt.	
Merrow, Sam'l	Rochester
Sam'l Jr.	Rochester
Messer, Richard	Salem
Metcalf, Abijah	Keene
Eli	Keene
Joseph	Chesterfield

Metcalf - Cont'd	
Jotham	Keene
Michael	Keene
Nathan	Chesterfield
Methes; see also Mathes;	
Benj.	Allenstown
Mighels, John, n.	Newmarket
Josiah, n.	Newmarket
Samuel, n.	Newmarket
Samuel Jr., n.	Newmarket
Miles, Abner	Canterbury
Arch^a Arch a	Canterbury
Henry	Winchester
Josiah	Canterbury
Josiah Jr.	Sanbornton
Samuel	Canterbury
William	Canterbury
Miller, Benjamin	Newington
Benjamin Jr.	Portsmouth
Heber, s.	Westmoreland
Hugh	Chester
James	Candia
James	Londonderry
John	Windham
Lamuel, n.	Alstead
Mark	Newington
Mathew	Londonderry
Moses	Portsmouth
Samuel	Londonderry
Samuel Jr.	Peterborough
Samuel Sr.	Peterborough
Samuel 3d	Peterborough
William	Chester
William	Peterborough
Milliken, Alexander	Wilton
Millington, Samuel	Lebanon
Solomon	Lebanon
Mills, Amos	Atkinson
J.	Nottingham
Jacob	Portsmouth
John	Chester
John, n.	Hampstead
Joseph	Deering
Reuben	Atkinson

Mills - Cont'd	
Rich'd	Portsmouth
Robert	Deering
Thomas	Dunbarton
William	Chester
Miltimer,	
William	Londonderry
Miltimor, Daniel	Society Land
James	Londonderry
Miltmor, James	Londonderry
Miner, Thomas	Canaan
Mitchal, David Jr.	Newcastle
Mitchel, Benj.	Peterborough
Dan'l (Rev.) n.	Pembroke
Jno.	Peterborough
Sam'l	Peterborough(2)
Thomas	Londonderry
Mitchell, Francis	Londonderry
Isaac	Peterborough
James	Concord
John	Amherst
Mixer, Timothy	Peterborough
Mody, Jonathan Jr.	Brentwood
Moffatt, John	Portsmouth
Molony, James	Canterbury
John	Canterbury
Molten, see Moulton.	
Monson, Richard	Portsmouth
Montgomary,	
Jonathan	Barrington
Montgomery,	
Hugh	Londonderry
John	Barrington
Moody, Moodey; see also Mody;	
Daniel	Unity
Elisha	Concord
John	Gilmanton
John	Newmarket
Josiah	Unity
Richard	Unity
Mooers,	
Edm'd	Hampstead
Parker	Londonderry
Sam'l	Candia

Moor, Allan, n.	New Boston	Moore - Cont'd	
Daniel	Bedford	William	Peterborough
Daniel Jr.	Bedford	William	Stratham
David	Bedford	William Sr.	Stratham
Ephraim	Bow	William 3d, n.	Stratham
George	Londonderry	Moores,	
James	Bow	John Jr.	Canterbury
John	Acworth	Sam'l	Society Land
John (Lt.)	Bedford	Moors, James	Society Land
John	Bedford	Mordogh, Nathan	Wakefield
John Jr.	Bedford	Moreson,	
John	Bow	Samuel	Londonderry
John	Canterbury	Morgain, Simeon	Brentwood
John	Londonderry	Morgan, Ashby	Wilton
John, n.	Londonderry	Cornelius	Chester
John	Pembroke (2)	Jeremiah	Pembroke
Robert	Londonderry	Josiah	New Boston
Robert, n.	Londonderry	Nathanael	Hopkinton
Robert	Pembroke	Morgen, Benj., n.	Epping
Samuel	Derryfield	Morgin, Reuben	Northwood
Samuel	Nottingham West	Moriel,	
Solomon, V. D. M.	New Boston	Nathaniel Jr.	Northwood
William	Bedford (2)	Morison,	
William	Canterbury	Abraham, n.	Londonderry
William	Londonderry	David, n.	Londonderry
William, n.	New Boston	John	Windham
William	Wakefield	Joseph	Londonderry
Moore,		Joseph Jr.	Londonderry
Archelaus	Canterbury	Robt.	Londonderry
Benjamin	Rindge	Samuel	Londonderry
Charles	Chester	Samuel Jr.	Londonderry
Charles Jr.	Chester	Sam'l	Windham
Harvey	Stratham	Thos.	Londonderry
James	Bedford	Thomas	Peterborough
John	Candia	William	Londonderry
John	Londonderry	Morland, Moorland,	
John, n.	Portsmouth	James	Salem
Joshua	Candia	John	Salem
Nathaniel	Canterbury	William	Salem
Peter, n.	Stratham	Morrel; see also Morrill;	
Samael	Chester	Robert	Bedford
S'll	Peterborough	Morriel; see also Moriel;	
Thomas, n.	Stratham	Paul	Loudon
Thomas (Cor.) n., Stratham		Morriell, Moses	Loudon

Morrill; see also Morrel;		Morrison - Cont'd	
Abel	Brentwood	Sam., n.	Henniker
Abraham	Brentwood	Sam'l	Sanbornton
Adonijah	Seabrook	Thos. Jr.	Peterborough
Barns	Londonderry	William	Rye
David	Canterbury	Morroson,	
Ephraim	Gilmanton	Ebenezer	Sanbornton
Ephraim Jr.	Gilmanton	Morrow,	
Ephraim	Henniker	Alexander	Windham
Ezekiel	Canterbury	John	Windham
Ezekiel	Loudon	Mors, Asa	Salem
Henry	Hawke	William	Deerfield
Isaac	Loudon	Morse, Daniel	Dublin
Jabez	Weare	Eli	Dublin
Jeremiah	East Kingston	Ezra	Dublin
John	Boscawen	Henry	Chester
John	East Kingston	John	Dublin
Joseph	Gilmanton	John	Packersfield
Joseph	Nottingham	Jonathan	Temple
Laben	Canterbury	Moses	Boscawen
Levi	Brentwood	Nathan	Chester
Maston	Loudon	Reuben	Dublin
Micajah	Hampton	Stephen	Chester
Nath'l	Northwood	Thos	Dublin
Obadiah	Chesterfield	Tho.	Gilsum
Oliver	Epping	Thomas	Pembroke
Robie	Boscawen	Morss, Abner	East Kingston
Samuel	Candia	Benj.	Exeter
Samuel	Epping	Edmund (Left.), n.,	
Sam'l	Epping		Hampstead
Samuel	Loudon	Joseph	Chester
Sargent	Canterbury	Joshua	Hopkinton
Simeon	Londonderry	Josiah	Chester
William	Brentwood	Moody	Salem
Morrison, Marison; see also		Moses Jr.	Boscawen
Moreson, Morison;		Parker	Chester
Abraham	Rochester	Peter	Hampstead
David	Canterbury	Peter, n.	Hampstead
John	Bedford	Samuel	Chester
John	Peterborough	Moses, Aaron	Portsmouth
Jonathan	Rochester	James	Portsmouth
Robt.	Londonderry	John	Portsmouth
Robert	Nottingham	Mark	Epsom
Robt.	Peterborough	Nadab	Portsmouth

Moses - Cont'd		Mudget, John	Barnstead
Samuel	Epsom	John	Weare
Samu'l	Portsmouth	Nicholas	Brentwood
Silvanus	Epsom	Simeon	Gilmanton
Theodore	Portsmouth	Thomas, n.	Gilmanton
Thomas	Portsmouth	Mudgit, Eben	Weare
Timothy	Lee	Scribner	Gilmanton
Moulton, Molten,		Mugate, John	Barnstead
Benj.	Hampton	Joseph	Barnstead
Benjamin	Kensington	Mump, Jacob	Richmond
Daniel	Rye	Muncey, David, n.	Lee
David	Hampton	Muncy, Timthey	Lee
David	Sandown	Murray, Daniel	Hopkinton
David	Weare	Murry, Beriah	Claremont
Edward B.	Hampton	Sam'l	Rye
Elisha	Hampton	Mussey,	
Ephraim	Hampton	Dimond	Amherst
Ezekiel	Hampton	Reuben, s.	Amherst
John	Hampton (2)	Muzey, John	Boscawen
John Jr.	Hampton	Muzzey,	
John 3rd	Hampton	John Esq., n.	Hampstead
John 5th	Hampton	John	Weare
John 6th	Hampton	Thomas, n.	Hampstead
Jon'a	Hampton	Muzzy, Benjamen	Raby
Jonathan Jr.	Hampton	John	Dublin
Jos.	Hampton	Joseph	Boscawen
Joseph	Loudon	Samuel	Boscawen
Joseph	North Hampton	Thomas	Dublin
Joseph Jr.	North Hampton	Nase, James	Kingston
Joseph	Portsmouth	Nason, Richard	Hawke
Josiah	Hampton	William	Epsom
Josiah Jr.	Hampton	Nay, John	Hampton
Nathan	Hampton	Joseph	Hampton
Nehemiah	Rye	Samuel	Hampton
Reuben	Rye	Neal,	
Robert	Gilmanton	Ebenezer	North Hampton
Robert	Hampton	Hubartus	Newmarket
Small	Hampton	Hubartus Jr.	Newmarket
Thomas	Deerfield	James	Newcastle
William	Hampstead	John, n.	Newmarket
William	Hampton	Samuel	Newmarket
Mountford, Tim'y	Portsmouth	Walter	Newmarket
Muchamore,		William	Newcastle
Nath'l	Portsmouth	Zebulon, n.	Newmarket

Neale,	
Hubartus	Exeter
Nealey, Andrew	Deerfield
Neall, Robert	Portsmouth
Nealley, John	Nottingham
Joseph, n.	Nottingham
Nelley, John Jr.	Nottingham
William	Nottingham
Nelson, Neson,	
James	Epsom
John	Barnstead
Leader	Portsmouth
Mark	Portsmouth
William	Keene
William	Portsmouth
Nesmith, James	Londonderry
James Jr.	Londonderry
John	Londonderry (2)
Neson, see Nelson.	
Nevens, David	Salem
Newel, Joseph	Richmond
Newell, Jacob	Monadnock
Newhall, John	Packersfield
Newman,	
Benjamin	Rindge
Thomas	Derryfield
Newmarch,	
Benjamin	Portsmouth
Newton,	
Ebenezer	Keene
Elnathan	Monadnock
Isaac	Newport
John	Kingston
Phinehes	Croydon
Robart	Winchester
Nichols, Asaph	Keene
Humphry	Hampstead
James	Brentwood
John	Hillsborough
Joseph	Kingston
Moses	Amherst
Samuel	Lempster
Timothy	Amherst
Timoth	Lempster

Nickels,	
Joseph	Hopkinton
Nickols, James	Londonderry
Jonathan	Packersfield
Nicoles,	
Alexander, n.	Londonderry
Nims, David	Keene
David Jr.	Keene
Eliakim	Keene
Zadock	Keene
Noble, John	Portsmouth
Mark	Portsmouth
Moses, n.	Portsmouth
Thomas	Lee
Norcrose,	
Jeremiah	Rindge
Norcross,	
Jeabez	Rindge
Page	Rindge
Norris, Noris,	
Benj. (Capt.) n.	Pembroke
David	Canterbury
David	Epping
James	Epping
James 4th	Epping
Joseph	Portsmouth
Joseph	Stratham
Josiah	Epping
Samuel	Portsmouth
Simeon	Epping
Thomas, n.	Epping
Zabulon	Northwood
Norton, John	Portsmouth
Jonathan	Chester
Joseph	Chester
Joseph, n.	Claremont
Joseph	Seabrook
Nathan	Chester
Norwood,	
Francis	Richmond
Francis Jr.	Richmond
Nott, Thos.	Acworth
Noyes; see also Nase;	
Aaron	Bow

Noyes - Cont'd		Nutter - Cont'd	
Benj.	Bow	Nelson Downing	Newington
Cutting	Boscawen	Rich'd	Rochester
Daniel	Boscawen	Valintine	Portsmouth
Daniel	Hopkinton	Oak, Nathanil	Winchester
Daniel	Pembroke	Oakes, Sam'l	Portsmouth
Enoch	Atkinson	Ober, Isarel	Salem
Enoch	Bow	Jacob, n.	New Boston
Humphery	Atkinson	O'Connor, see also Connor;	
Humphery Jr.	Atkinson	John Thing	Hopkinton
Isaac	Boscawen	Joseph	Hopkinton
James	Atkinson	Odel, Thomas	Nottingham
John	Bow	Thomas	Stratham
John	Kingston	Odell, Joseph	Conway
Joseph	Atkinson	William	Amherst
Joseph	Hampstead	William Jr.	Amherst
N.	South Hampton	Odiorne, John	Newcastle
Nathaniel	Atkinson	Samuel	Newcastle
Samuel	Atkinson	William, n.	Epsom
Samuel	Pembroke	William, n.	Newmarket
Stephen	Atkinson	Odlin, Elisha	Gilmanton
Thomas	Atkinson	Will'm	Exeter
Nudd, James	North Hampton	Ordway, Ardway,	
John	North Hampton	Jacob	East Kingston
Samuel	Canterbury	John	Lebanon
Simon	Hampton	John	Weare
Thomas	Hampton	Joseph	Salem
Nurs, Benjamen	Packersfield	Moses	Loudon
Nurse, Benjmin Jr.	Packersfield	Nathan	East Kingston
Nute, John	Rochester	Samuel	Weare
Samuel	Rochester	Ormsbe, Ornsbe,	
Nutt, William	Derryfield	Ebenezer	Richmond
Nuton, William	Salisbury	Ezra	Richmond
Nutter, Benja.	Barnstead	Oliver	Richmond
Christopher	Newington	Orr, George	Londonderry
Hatevil	Barnstead	Hugh	Bedford
Hatevil	Newington	John	Bedford
Hatevil 3d	Newington	John	Chester
Henry	Portsmouth (2)	Osborn,	
James	Newington (2)	Jonathan, Q	Weare
John	Newington	Osgood, Ozgood,	
Joseph	Newington	Benjamin	Conway
Joshua	Newington	Benjamin	Keene
Jotham	Rochester	Benjamin Jr., n.	Keene

Osgood - Cont'd	
Chase	Epping
James	Epping
John	Conway
Joseph	Gilmanton
Joshua	Keene
Moses	Epsom
Nathaniel	Deerfield
Philip	South Hampton
Rebben	Epping
Samuel	Gilmanton
William	Claremont
Otes, Joshua	Barrington
Micajah	Barrington
Nicholes	Barrington
Stephen	Barrington
Otis, Elijah	Barrington
Paul	Barrington
Owen, Daniel	Winchester
Packerd, Joseph	Westmoreland
Padelford,	
Jonathan	Enfield
Jonathan Jr.	Enfield
Phillip	Enfield
Page, Paig,	
Aaron	Kensington
Abner	Hampton
Abr'a	Nottingham West
Abraham	Londonderry
Asa	Atkinson
Benjamin	Deerfield
Benjamin	Epping
Benjamin	Hampton
Benjamin	Weare
Caleb	Dunbarton
Caleb Jr.	Dunbarton
Daniel	Atkinson
Daniel	Deerfield
Dan'l	Rochester
Daniel	South Hampton
Daniel, Q	Weare
David	Conway
David	North Hampton
David Jr.	North Hampton

Page - Cont'd	
Ebenezer, n.	Salem
Eli	Richmond
Enoch	Nottingham
Enock	South Hampton
Frances	North Hampton
Henry	Sandown
Isaac	Londonderry
Jabez	Hawke
James	Atkinson
James	Deerfield
Jeremiah	Conway
Jeremiah	Dunbarton
Jeremiah	Epsom
Jeremiah	North Hampton
Jeremiah	Sandwich
Jeremiah	Weare
Jesse	Atkinson
John	Epping
John	Hawke
John	Kensington
John Jr.	Kensington
John	Rindge
John	Sandwich
Jonathan	Atkinson
Jonathan Jr.	Atkinson
Jonathan	Hampstead
Jon'a	North Hampton
Jonathan	Sandwich
Joseph	Rochester
Joseph	Seabrook
Josiah	Wakefield
Moses	Atkinson
Moses	Epping
Nathan, Q	Kensington
Nathaniel	Rindge
Onesiphorus	South Hampton
Reuben	Londonderry
Reuben	Rindge
Robert	Deerfield
Robert	Seabrook
Samuel	Hampton
Samuel	North Hampton
Samuel	Rindge

Page - Cont'd	
Samuel Jr.	Rindge
Shubel	Hampton
Simon	Kensington
Simon	North Hampton
Stephen	Atkinson
Stephen	Hampton
Stephen	Kensington
Stephen	North Hampton
Theophilus, Q	Kensington
Thomas	Hampton
Thomas	Hawke
William	Dunbarton
William	Londonderry
Paige, Andrew	Gilmanton
Ebenezer	Gilmanton
Jonathan	Weare
Lemuel	Weare
Samuel	Weare
Samuel Jr.	Weare
Pain, Amos	Chester
John	Chester
Philip, n.	Gilmanton
Paine, Amos, n.	Gilmanton
Samuel	Lebanon
Pallet, Joseph	Canterbury
Nathaniel	Canterbury
Palmer; see also	Pulmmer;
Barn's	Rochester
Benjamin	North Hampton
Cotton, n.	Portsmouth
Jacob	Hampton
Jonathan	Atkinson
Jonathan	Kensington
Jon'a	Wakefield
Joseph	Atkinson
Joseph	Candia
Joseph	Leavitt's Town
Joseph	North Hampton
Philbrick	Kensington
Samuel	East Kingston
Stephen	Candia
Stephen Jr.	Candia
Stephen, n.	Dunbarton

Palmer - Cont'd	
Thomas Jr.	Portsmouth
Trueworthy	East Kingston
William	Leavitt's Town
William	Portsmouth
Parcely,	
Richard	Barrington
Parham, John	Derryfield
William	Derryfield (2)
Park, Alex'dr	Windham
Alexander Jr.	Windham
Andrew	Windham
Phinehas	Monadnock
Robert	Windham
Parker,	
Alexander	Society Land
Benjamin	Wilton
Eben	Atkinson
Ezra	Winchester
Henry	Wilton
Jn'o.	Portsmouth
Johnthan	Claremont
Jonth	Rindge
Jon'a Jr.	Rindge
Joseph	Pembroke
Josiah	Wilton
Noah, n.	Portsmouth
Peter	Amherst
Reuben	Richmond
Robert	Lee
Sam'l, n.	Pembroke
Sam'l	Rindge
Wm.	Londonderry
William	Portsmouth (2)
Parkhurst, Jon'a.	Wilton
Parkins, Joseph	Wakefield
Parkinson,	
William	Londonderry
Parlin, Stephen	Temple
Parmele, Ezra	Newport
Parsely, John	Barrington
Parshley,	
George	Barrington
Parson, Daniel	Weare

Parsons,	
Abraham	Newmarket
Jacob, n.	Newmarket
Job	Epping
Jno.	Gilmanton
Joseph	Gilmanton
Joseph	Rye
Samuel	Epping
Thos.	Leavitt's Town
William	Gilmanton
William Jr.	Gilmanton
Partridge, Benj.	Portsmouth
Levi	Dublin
Reuben	Keene
William	Portsmouth
Patee, Edward	Salem
Jerediah	Londonderry
Seth	Salem
Zephaniah	Concord
Paten, Nathell	Raby
Patten, John	Exeter
John	Temple
Matthew	Bedford
Robert	Chester
Samuel	Bedford (2)
Samuel	Deering
Thomas	Candia
William	Kingston
Patterson, Adem	Amherst
Alexander	Henniker
Alexander	New Boston
Benj.	Piermont
Ephraim	Piermont
Isaac	Piermont
James	Bedford
John	Amherst
John	Londonderry
John	Piermont
Nathaniel	Bedford
Robert, n.	New Boston
Robert Jr.	New Boston
Robert 3d	New Boston
Thomas	Londonderry
William	Wilton

Pattinson,	
Joseph (Capt.) n., Newington	
Patton, John	Londonderry
Paul, David	Londonderry
James	Londonderry
Payn[?], Nathaniel Epsom	
Peabody, Pebody,	
David	Londonderry
Eph'm	Wilton
Isaac	Londonderry
Isaac Sr.	Wilton
Isaac Jr.	Wilton
Nath'l	Atkinson
Stephen	Amherst
Stephen	Atkinson
Thos.	Brentwood
William	Amherst
William Jr.	Amherst
Peacock, John	Chesterfield
John	Hinsdale
Sam'l	Chesterfield
William	Amherst
Peake, John	Claremont
Pearce; see also Pearse, Peirce,	
Perce, Pierce, Pirce;	
James	Chester
Pearl,	
Abraham, n. Rochester	
Diamond	Rochester
Jos'h	Rochester
Pearne,	
Will'm	Portsmouth
Pearse, Peter, n. Portsmouth,	
absent at Newington.	
Pearson, Isaac Boscawen	
John	Deerfield
John	Kingston
Joseph	Boscawen
Oliver	Hopkinton
Peas, Nathel	Newmarket
Pease,	
Benjamin, n. Newmarket	
Eliphelet	Newmarket
John	Epping

Pease - Cont'd
Joseph	Newmarket
Nathaniel	Barnstead
Pelatiah	Gilsum
Sam'l	Newmarket

Peaslee,
Benj., Q	Weare
Caleb, Q	Weare
Ebenezer, Q	Weare
Jonathan, Q	Weare
Nath'l, Q	Weare
Silas, Q	Weare

Peasley, Pesly,
Daniel Esq., n.	Salem
Jacob	Kingston

Peavey, Hutson	Newington
James	Barrington
Peavy, Joeph	Barrington
Peck, Walter	Lebanon
Peevey, Thomas	Rochester
Peirce, Amos	Westmoreland
Benjamin	Rindge
Benjamin	Westmoreland
Dan'l	Portsmouth
Daniel	Westmoreland
Eben'er	Westmoreland
Humphry	South Hampton
Humpheery Jr.	South Hampton
John	Portsmouth
John (merch't) n.	n., Portsmouth
John, n.	Winchester
John Jr.	Winchester
Joseph	Amherst
Moses	South Hampton
Noah	Portsmouth
Samuel	South Hampton
Thos.	Portsmouth
Thomas Jr.	Portsmouth
William	Wilton
Peirse, James	Derryfield
Pendell, Elisha	Gilsum
Pendexter, Edward	Portsmouth
John	Conway
Phillip	Portsmouth

Penhallow,
John	Portsmouth
R. Wibird	Portsmouth
Sam'l	Portsmouth

Pepperrill, A.	Portsmouth
Perce, Benjamin	Chester

Perkins, Parkines, Pearkins,
Perkines, Pirkins, Pur-
kins; see also Parkins;
Abel	Rindge
Abraham	Epping
Abraham Jr.	Epping
Barnabas	Lebanon
Benjamin	Wakefield
Daniel	Seabrook
David	Epping
Elisha	Rindge
James	Hampton
James, n.	Keene
James	Rye
James Lind	Canterbury
John Jr.	Epping
John	Lempster
John	Newmarket (2)
Jonathan	East Kingston
Jonathan	Kensington
Joseph	Salem
Joseph, Q	Weare
Limuel	Barrington
Moses	Newmarket
Nathaniel	Canterbury
Richard, n.	Newmarket
Samuel	Deerfield
Simon	Weare
Solo.	Rochester
Solo. Jr.	Rochester
Thomas	Wakefield
Timothy	Barrington
True	East Kingston
William, n.	Newmarket
Perl, Ben—	Barrington

Perley,
Samuel, V. D. M.	Seabrook
Perrin, Thomas	Londonderry

Perry, Pery,
 Abijah Wilton
 David Winchester
 Ebenezer Wilton
 Ivory Dublin
 Jonas Wilton
Pervere, John Sandown
Pervier,
 James Noies Seabrook
Pesly, see Peasley.
Peters; see also Petters;
 Daniel Richmond
 Ebenezer Richmond
 Isrel Richmond
 James Henniker
 Richard Richmond
 Richard Jr. Richmond
Peterson,
 Benjamin, n. Claremont
 Daniel Boscawen
 Willet Kingston
Pettengill, Abbit Salem
 Andrew Salisbury
 David Salisbury
 Matthew Salisbury
Petters, William Hopkinton
Pettingell, Ephrain Epsom
Peverly, Kinsman Portsmouth
 William Portsmouth
Phelps, Joseph Wilton
 Josha Pembroke
Philbrick,
 Benjamin Atkinson
 Benjamin Jr. Atkinson
 Benjamin North Hampton
 Daniel, n. Hampton
 Daniel Jr. Hampton
 Elias Northwood
 James Hampton
 James Rindge
 Jedidiah Hawke
 John Brentwood (2)
 John Deerfield
 John Hampton

Philbrick - Cont'd
 Jonathan Deerfield
 Jonathan Epping
 Jonathan Rye
 Joseph Hampstead
 Joseph Hampton
 Joseph Rye
 Nathan Deerfield
 Nathaniel Deerfield
 Reuben Rye
 Samuel Hampton
 Sam'l Kingston
 Sam'el Weare
 Titus Rye
Philbrook,
 Benjamin Wakefield
 Eliphalet Wakefield
Philips, Israel Richmond
Phillips, James Packersfield
Pickerin, Daniel Stratham
Pickering,
 Anthony, n. Newmarket
 Ephermim Newington
 James Newington
 John Portsmouth
 Rich'd Newington
 Winthrop Newington
Pickern, Nicholas Newington
Pickett,
 Giles, n. Portsmouth
Pickreing,
 Benjamin Newington
 John Gee Newington
 Levi Newmarket
 Thomas Newington
Pickren, Stephen Barnstead
Pickreng, John Newington
Pierce; see also Pearce, Pearse,
  Peirce, Perce, Pierce,
  Pirce;
 John Chesterfield
Piercy, Richard Bourke,
   Peterborough
Pike, John Epping

Pike - Cont'd	
John	Portsmouth
Joshua	Portsmouth
Nath'll	Portsmouth
Robert	Kensington
Robert	Newmarket
Pillar, Thomas	Portsmouth
Pillsbery, Ezra	Weare
Pilsbery,	
Benjamin	Sandown
Caleb	Loudon
Edmund	Brentwood
Joh	South Hampton
Pilsbury,	
Edmund	South Hampton
Jonathan	Candia
Moses	Loudon
Pinder, Thomas	Newington
Pindexter, see Pendexter.	
Pinkerton, David	Londonderry
John	Londonderry (2)
Mathew	Londonderry
Pinkham, Abijah	Barrington
Jonathan	Rochester
Piper, Benj.	Newmarket
Benj.	Pembroke
Benjamin, n.	Stratham
Elisha	Wakefield
Gideon	Pembroke
John	Stratham
Jonathan	Stratham
Jonathan Jr.	Stratham
Nathaniel, n.	Stratham
Samuel	Stratham
Samuel Jr.	Stratham
Stephen, n.	Stratham
Thomas, n.	Newmarket
Thomas	Northwood
Pirce, James, n.	Hinsdale
Samuel	Chester
Pirkins, see Perkins.	
Pitcher, Gorge	Kingston
Pitman,	
Ebenezer	Meredith

Pitman - Cont'd	
Ezekiel	Portsmouth
John	Portsmouth
Joseph	Lee
Joseph	Portsmouth
Nath	Portsmouth
Samuel	Barnstead
Place, Eben'r	Rochester
Eben'r Jr.	Rochester
George	Rochester
John	Rochester
Rich'd	Rochester
Plats,	
Abell Jr.	Rindge
Joseph	Rindge
Platts, Abel	Rindge
Plumbley, John	Alstead
Plumer, Bitfield	Boscawen
Jesse	Londonderry
Samuel	Epping
Weanslo	Londonderry
Plummer, Abel	Londonderry
Beard	Rochester
John, n.	Hampstead
John	Rochester
Joseph	Rochester
Kelley, n.	Hampstead
Sam'l	Rochester
Thomas	Rochester
Pollard, Pallerd,	
Amaziah	Bedford
Amos	Nottingham West
John Jr.	Nottingham West
Jonathan	Kingston
Joseph	Nottingham West
Pollerd,	
Samuel	Nottingham West
Polord, John	Nottingham West
Obenezer	Nottingham West
Timothey	Nottingham West
Pomeroy,	
Eleazer, n.	Chesterfield
Pomroy, Josiah (Dr.), n.,	
	Keene

Pond, Abithar	Keene	Prentice – Cont'd	
Poor, Daniel	Atkinson	Nath'l S.	Alstead
Daniel Jr.	Atkinson	Solomon	Alstead
David	Hampstead	Presbe, Edward	Dunbarton
Eliph't	Hampstead	Prescot, Joshua	Chester
Jer'h	Atkinson	Prescott, Pruscott,	
Jona	Atkinson	Benj.	Kensington
Pope, David	Henniker	Henry	Newcastle
Thomas	Henniker	James	Candia
William	Hillsborough	Jedidiah Jr.	Deerfield
Porter, David	Londonderry	Jeremiah	Epping
Nathaniel	Lebanon	Jeremiah	Epsom
Nat'l Jr.	Lebanon	John	Candia
Nehemiah	Rindge	John, n.	Deerfield
Potter, Eben'r	Kensington	John	Epping
Ephraim	Concord	Jonathan	Epping
Isaiah	Lebanon	Jon'a	Kensington
John	North Hampton	Joseph	Epping (2)
Richard	Concord	Josiah	Deerfield
Pottle, Pottel,		Marston	Kensington
Samuel, n.	Stratham	Odlin	Kensington
William	Stratham	William	Northwood
Wm. Jr.	Stratham	Prescut, Priescut,	
Poudney; see also Putney;		Edward	Hampstead
Henery	Dunbarton	Jesse	Deerfield
Powel, Moses, n.	Henniker	John	Sandwich
Powers,		Micah	Epping
Benjamin	Croydon	Nathan Gove	Epping
David	Croydon	Prescutt,	
Eliot	Temple	Abraham	Deerfield
Ezekiel	Chesterfield	Abraham	Kensington
Ezekiel, n.	Croydon	Joshua	Sandwich
Giddeon	Temple	Nathan	Brentwood
John, n.	Croydon	Samuel	Deerfield
Stephen	Croydon	Samuel	Kensington
William	Henniker	Simon	Kensington
Prasa, Jon'a	South Hampton	Stephen	East Kingston
Prat, John	Chesterfield	Preson,	
Pratt, Jeremiah	Winchester	Nathan, n.	Newmarket
Moses	Dublin	Pressey; see also Prasa;	
Preast; see also Priest;		Charles	Sandown
Quick	Nottingham	Preston,	
Prentice; see also Printice;		Jedidiah	Hillsborough
John	Londonderry	Samuel	Hillsborough

Pridham, Isaac	Newcastle		Putney; see also Poudney,	
Priest; see also Preast;			Pudney;	
Thomas	Portsmouth		Asa	Dunbarton
Prince, Joseph	Amherst		Asa	Henniker
Joseph Jr.	Amherst		John	Hopkinton
Printice,			Joseph	Hopkinton
Joseph, n.	Chesterfield		Quemby,	
Prissen, Edward	Chester		James	Meredith
Procter, James	Kingston		Samuel	Exeter
Jon'a	Kingston		William	Weare
Thomas	Kingston		Quenbe, Aaron	Weare
Pruscott, see Prescott.			Joseph	Weare
Pudney, John	Henniker		Quinbe, Moses	Weare
Puff(?), John	Portsmouth		Quimby, Aaron	Hawke
Puffer, Elijeh	Peterborough		Eliphalet	Wakefield
Jabe	Dublin		John	Brentwood
Pulmmer, Samuel	Sandown		John	Chester
Pulsfer, Samuel	Deerfield		Moses	Hawke
Pulsifer,			Samuel	Hawke
Benjamin	Brentwood		Timothy	Kingston
Purinton, Purintun,			Quinby,	
Elijah, Q	Weare		Benjamin	Hopkinton
Hezekiah, Q	Weare		David	Hawke
Jonathan, Q	Kensington		Jonathan	Brentwood
Purmort,			Jonatha	Hopkinton
Richeard	Salisbury		Jonathan	Hopkinton
Puruy, Aaron	Hinsdale		Tristram	Kingston
Putmen, Benjamin	Dunbarton		Quint, Benj.	Portsmouth
Putnam,			Jonathan	Portsmouth
Andrew	Winchester		Racklyft,	
Archelas, n.	Wilton		Roger, n.	Newmarket
Archelaus Jr.	Wilton		Raley, Philip	Society Land
Caleb	Wilton		Ramsdell, see Remsdell.	
Jacob, n.	Temple		Ramsey, Hugh	New Boston
Jacob	Wilton		James	Londonderry
Jacob Jr.	Wilton		John	Londonderry (2)
John	Lee		William	Londonderry
Jonathan	Rindge		Ran, David	Sanbornton
Joseph, n.	Temple		Ranar, James	Richmond
Nathaniel	Wilton		Rand, Benjman	Saville
Philip	Wilton		Daniel	Rindge
Stephen	Temple		Ezekiel	Rindge
Stephen	Winchester		John	Derryfield
Thos.	Acworth		John	Rye (2)

Rand - Cont'd

Josep	Rye
Joseph	Rye
Lemuel	Gilmanton
Nathanel	Rye
Nathenill	Rye
Samuel	Epsom
Samuel	Rye
Solomon	Rindge
Thos.	Deerfield
William	Epsom

Randall, George Rye

James	Chester
Joses	Stratham
Mark	Rye
Paul	Newcastle

Randel,

Ebenezer	Lee
Hezekiah	Nottingham
Israel	Nottingham
Miles	Lee
Nathanel	Nottingham

Randell, John Hampton

John	Rochester

Randul,

Abraham	Richmond

Ranken, Renkin,

James	Chester
Samuel	Londonderry
Will'm	Londonderry

Ranney,

Thos. Stow Hawke
Ransom, Thomas Portsmouth
Ranstead, John Westmoreland
Rawlians, Stephen Northwood
Rawlings, Benj. Salem

Jonathan	Stratham
Joseph	Newington
Noah, n.	Newington
Paul	Newington
Samuel	Newington

Rawlins, Jos. Exeter

Joshua	Stratham
Jotham	Sanbornton

Rawllins,

Jotham	Stratham

Rawlige,

Eliphalet	Loudon

Ray, Abel Chesterfield

John	Derryfield

Rayner, see Ranar.
Razey, Joseph Richmond
Rea, Ebene'r Amherst
Read, Daniel Richmond

Micah	Westmoreland
Robert	Amherst
William	Amherst

Readman, John Hampton
Reddell, James Bow
Redding, Thomas Surry
Redman,

Tristram	North Hampton

Reed,

Abraham (Lieut), n.,
     Windham

Benjamin	Portsmouth
George	Portsmouth
James	Chesterfield
John, n.	Londonderry
John	Portsmouth
Jonathan	Londonderry
Mathew, n.	Windham

Reith(?), John, n. Salem
Remick, Enoch Newmarket
Remsdell, Jacob Weare
Rendal, Moses Sanbornton
Rendel, Mason Nottingham

Simon	Lee

Renels; see also Runals, Runels;

Isaac	Barrington
John	Barrington

Rest, Philip Godfrid Hopkinton
Reynolds,

Jedediah	Newport
Jed'h Jr.	Newport

Rice, Charls Surry

Daniel	Henniker
Elijah	Henniker

Rice - Cont'd

Elijah	Rindge
Jacob	Claremont
Jacob	Henniker
Micah	Sandwich
Peter	Keene
Rich, David	Claremont
Josiah	Claremont

Richards,

Benjamin	Atkinson
Bradlee	Atkinson
Daniel	Atkinson
Daniel	Boscawen
John	Piermont
John	Rochester
John Jr.	Rochester
Jonathan	Rochester
Joseph	Temple
William	Portsmouth

Richardson; see also Ritcherson;

Daniel	Chester
David	Chester
James	Chester
Jephthah	Rindge
Jeremi	Gilmanton
John	Chesterfield
John	Hampstead
Joseph	Temple
Josiah	Keene
Lemuel	Rochester
Moses	Chester
Paul, n.	Winchester
Pearson	Chester
Perish	Acworth
William Jr.	Hampstead
William	Londonderry
Richey, Alexd'r	Windham
Alexander Jr.	Windham
James	Peterborough
James	Windham
Richmond, Zeph'h	Hinsdale
Ricker, Eben'r	Rochester

Riddle; see also Reddell;

| John | Bedford |

Rideout, Benj.	Wilton
Rider, Ebenezer	Hopkinton
Riggs, Thos.	Monadnock
Right, Joseph	Winchester
Oliver	Dublin
Rindge, Isaac, n.	Portsmouth
Ring, Jonathan	Candia
Rins, Josiah	Loudon
Rinton, William	Newmarket

Ritcherson,

| William | Hampstead |

Roads,

| Ebenezer | Monadnock |

Robards, Robords,

Amaziah	Winchester
Benjamin	Brentwood
Samuel	Brentwood

Robbards,

| Richard | Monadnock |

Robbe,

Alexander	Peterborough
James	Peterborough
William	Peterborough

Robbins,

Benoni	Monadnock
David	Rindge
Eleazer	Westmoreland
Ephraim	Westmoreland
John	Westmoreland
Jonas	Westmoreland
William	Rindge

Robenson,

John (Capt.) n.	Deerfield
Joseph	Deering
Nath'l, n.	Deerfield

Roberds,

Alexander	Brentwood
Joseph	Meredith
Sander [Jr. ?]	Brentwood
Thomas	Brentwood

Roberson,

Archibald	Chesterfield
Elexander	Deering
Josiah, n.	Epping

Roberson - Cont'd		Robinson - Cont'd	
Simeon	Londonderry	Gideon	Meredith
Robert, Natha	Barrington	Gilman	Brentwood
Roberts, Moses	Rochester	James	Brentwood
Thomas	Rochester	James	Pembroke
Timothy	Rochester	Jedediah	Brentwood
Robertson,		John	Canterbury
And'w, n.	Pembroke	John	Deerfield
James	Chesterfield	John	Richmond
James	Pembroke	John	Sanbornton
John	Bow	John	Stratham
Peter	Amherst	Jonathan	Brentwood
Rob't	Portsmouth	Jonathan	Deerfield
Robert, n.	Portsmouth	Jonathan	Epping
Thos.	Pembroke	Jonathan Jr.	Epping
Will'm	Bow	Jonathan	Newmarket
William	Chesterfield	Jonathan	Stratham
William	Deering	Joseph	Nottingham
Will'm, n.	Pembroke	Nathaniel	Meredith
Robie; see also Roby;		Nichols	Epping
Edward	Chester (2)	Peter	Londonderry
Enoch	Deerfield	Peter	Pembroke
Henry	Seabrook	Sam'l	Rochester
Ichabod	Pembroke	Simeon	Canterbury
John	Candia	Simeon	Epping
John	Chester	Thomas	Epping
John	North Hampton	Thos.	Salem
John	Weare	Timothy	Richmond
Sam'l	Chester	Zebelon, n.	Pembroke
Samuel	North Hampton	Robison,	
Thomas	Deerfield	Alexander	Londonderry
Walter	Candia	John	Londonderry (2)
Robins, David	Westmoreland	Robords, see Robards.	
Douglass	Chesterfield	Roby; see also Robie;	
Eleaser Jr.	Westmoreland	John	Amherst
Robert	Westmoreland	Rockwood, Asa	Winchester
Robinson; see also Robenson;		Elisha	Chesterfield
Chas	Meredith	Micah	Hinsdale
David	Brentwood	Nath	Winchester
David	Deerfield	Reuben	Winchester
David	Stratham	Thos., n.	Hinsdale
David	Westmoreland	Roen, John	Canterbury
Dudley	Brentwood	Rogers, Abner	Hampstead
Eliezer	Lebanon	Benjamin	Westmoreland

Rogers – Cont'd
Daniel Esq., n.	Nottingham
Daniel	Portsmouth,
absent at Nottingham	
Daniel	Rochester
James	Acworth
James	Rochester
James Jr.	Rochester
James, Tertius	Rochester
John	Acworth
Joseph	Bow
Joseph Jr.	Bow
Josiah	South Hampton
Nathaniel, n.	Newmarket
Peter Jr.	Weare
Richard Carr	Hopkinton
Robert	Society Land
Samuel	Bow
Samuel Jr.	Bow
Stephen	South Hampton
Thomas	Londonderry
William	Bow
William	Londonderry
Rolens, Henery	Wakefield

Rolf, Rollf,
Daniel	Hillsborough
Janes	Raby

Rolfe, Benj. Boscawen
Benj.	Concord
Nath'l	Concord

Rolings; see also Rollings,
 Rowlings;
David	Barrington

Rolins; see also Rolens;
James	Dublin

Rollings,
Jonathan	Nottingham
Joseph	Amherst
Moses	Loudon

Rollins, Benj.	Rochester
Ich'd	Rochester
Root, Ephraim	Piermont
Ross, Jesse	Henniker
Jonathan	Gilmanton

Ross – Cont'd
Levi	Concord
Moses	Portsmouth
Timothy	Henniker

Rouel, see Rowel.

Roundye, Samuel Lempster

Row, Ichabod Nottingham
James	Barrington
John	Gilsum
John Jr.	Gilsum
John	Salisbury

Rowe, Aretas Brentwood
Benjamin	Kensington
Benjamin Jr.	Kensington
Isaiah	Candia
James	Gilsum
Jeremiah, n.	Brentwood
Jonathan	Kensington
Joseph	Kensington
Robert	Brentwood
Robert	Chester
Wintrop	Kensington

Rowel, Rouel,
Benjamin	Candia
Enoch	Candia
Gideon	Chester
Jacob, n.	Salem
Josiah	Salem
Josiah Jr., n.	Salem
Moses	Londonderry
Phillip, n.	Salem
Samuel	Chester
Sherbun	Candia
William	Sandown

Rowell,
Abraham	Hopkinton
Asa	Salem
Benoni	Salem
Christopher	Hampstead
Daniel	Barrington
Daniel	East Kingston
Jacob	East Kingston
John	Epping
Nathaniel	South Hampton

Rowell – Cont'd	
Nehemiah	Portsmouth
Rice	Nottingham
William	Windham
Rowlings; see also Rolings,	
Rollings;	
Aaron	Deerfield
Benj.	Epping
Nich's	Stratham
Thomos	Barrington
Royce, Samuel	Alstead
Roys,	
Ebenezer, n.	Claremont
Hezekiah, n.	Claremont
Joel	Claremont
Royse, Vere	Conway
Rudd, Gideon	Canaan
Rudman, Wm.	Lebanon
Rugg, Nathan	Keene
Rumrill, Henry	Alstead
Simon	Alstead
Runals, Job	Lee
Jonathan	Lee
Moses	Lee
Rundals, Daniel	Londonderry
Rundlet,	
Charles, n.	Lee
Daniel	Epping
Jacob	Epping
Jacob	Stratham
James	Epping (2)
James Jr., n.	Epping
John	Stratham
Josiah	Epping
Theo	Sanbornton
Rundlett,	
Jonathan	Epping
Rundletts,	
Charles	Portsmouth
Runels; see also Renels, Runals;	
Enoch	Lee
Job Jr.	Lee
William	Barrington
Russ, John	Derryfield

Russel, David	Richmond
George	Londonderry
Russell, Daniel	Rindge
Edw'd	Bow
Eleazer, n.	Portsmouth
George	Raby
Jer'ah	Rindge
Joel	Rindge
Joel Jr.	Rindge
Nathanael	Rindge
Samuell	Raby
Samuel	Rindge
Thomas	Conway
Thomas	Wilton
Wm	Rindge
Rust, Nathaniel	Alstead
Rich'd	Stratham
Ryan, James	Portsmouth
Sally, see Tally.	
Salter, Alaxander	Rye
Sambon, David	Kingston
Samborn, Aaron	Sanbornton
Daniel	North Hampton
Eben'r	North Hampton
John	East Kingston
John	Gilmanton
Joseph	Barnstead
Joseph	Canterbury
Josiah	Sanbornton (2)
Nathan	Epping
Nathan Jr.	Epping
Nathaniel	Epping
Thomas	North Hampton
William	Canterbury
William	North Hampton
Zadok	Brentwood
Sambun,	
Abraham	Kensington
Samburn, Nathan	Gilmanton
Sampson, Nathan	East Kingston
Samson, William	East Kingston
Sanbon, Daniel	Brentwood
Daniel Jr.	Brentwood
Edward	Epping

Sanbon - Cont'd		Sanborn - Cont'd	
Jonathan	Newmarket	Joseph	Brentwood
Moses	Sandown	Joseph	Wakefield
Sanborn, Abijah	Sanbornton	Joseph Clifford	Hawke
Abner	Hampton	Josiah, n.	Deerfield
Abraham	Kingston	Lowel	Gilmanton
Benjamin	Deerfield	Moses	Hopkinton
Beainjman	Kingston	Moses	Kensington
Benj.	Salisbury	Nathan	Deerfield
Benjamin	Sanbornton	Nathan	Hampton
Chandler	Epping	Peter	Deerfield
Daniel	Epping	Peter	Kingston
Dan'l	Sanbornton	Samuel	Sandown
David	Sandown	Sherburne	Sandown
Eben'r	Sanbornton	Simon	Hampton
Edward	Barnstead	Theophilus	Kensington
Edward	Brentwood	Timothy	Kingston
Eliph't	Epsom	Tristram	Deerfield
Elisha	Brentwood	William	Kingston
Elisha Jr.	Brentwood	Winthrop	Hampton
Henry	Northwood	Sanbun, Henry	Kensington
Isaac	Kingston	Reuben	Epsom
James	Epping	Sanburn, Benj.	Canterbury
James	Kensington (2)	Sandborn,	
Jeremiah	Epping	Abraham	Unity
Jeremiah	Hampton	Joseph	Newmarket
Jethro	Hawke	Sandboun,	
Jethro	Kingston	Richard	Kensington
Jethro	Sandown	Sander, John	Pembroke
John	Barnstead (2)	Sanders, Sonders,	
John	Canterbury	George	Epsom
John	East Kingston	James	Salem
John	Hampton	Joseph	Salem
John	Hawke	Robart	Rye
John	Kingston	Robert Jr.	Rye
John	Lee	Sam'l	Salem
John	Loudon	Stephen	Temple
John	Salisbury	Willan	Salem
John	Sandown	Sanderson, John	Chesterfield
Jonathan	Hampton	Sangar, Isaac	Croydon
Jonathan	Hawke	John	Croydon
Jonathan	Kingston	Sanger, Phinehas	Croydon
Jonathan Jr.	Kingston	Sangor, Abner n.	Keene
Jonathan	Northwood	Elezer, n.	Keene

Sargant, Isaac	Weare
Sargeant, Nathan	Hopkinton
Philip	Weare
Timothy	Salem
Sargent, Aaron	Canterbury
Abel	Dunbarton
Abraham	Chester
Charles	Londonderry
Chelas	Londonderry
David	Sandown
Enoch	Dunbarton (2)
Jacob	Weare
John	Candia (2)
John	Loudon
Mikl	Boscawen
Moses	Candia
Noah	Dunbarton
Peter	Hopkinton
Samuel	Hawke
Starlin	Allenstown
Trueworthy	Londonderry
Wintrup	Chester
Sarget, Thomas	Portsmouth
Saunders,	
Henry, n.	Salem
Oliver, n.	Salem
Savage, John	Portsmouth
Josiah	Portsmouth
Saveg, Job	Newmarket
Sawtell, Jonathan	Rindge
Sawyer,	
Benjamin	Hopkinton
Daniel, Q	Northwood
Enos	Piermont
Gideon	Canterbury
Gideon	Hawke
Israel	South Hampton
James	Hawke
Jesse	Atkinson
John	Hampstead
John	Piermont
Jonathan	Amherst
Jonathan	Atkinson
Jonathan	Westmoreland

Sawyer - Cont'd	
Joshua	Hampstead
Josiah	Amherst
Josiah Jr.	Amherst
Josiah	Deerfield
Josiah	South Hampton
Matthias	Gilmanton
Moses	Hopkinton
Mosses	Salisbury
Oliver	Atkinson
Oliver	Hopkinton
Richard	South Hampton
William	Atkinson
Scails,	
Abraham, n.	Nottingham
Samuel	Nottingham
Scales, Edward	Lee
James	Hopkinton
William	Hopkinton
Scamell, Daniel	Salisbury
Scammon,	
Richard, n.	Stratham
Schophel; see also Scofield;	
Thomas	Lempster
Thomas Jr.	Lempster
Scipio, Sol	Canaan
Scobey, David	New Boston
Scofield; see also Schophel;	
Eliezer	Canaan
John	Canaan
John Jr.	Canaan
Scott,	
Abraham	Winchester
Ebe'r	Winchester
Ebeneser Jr.	Winchester
Isaac	Winchester
John	Peterborough
John	Richmond
John	Westmoreland
Sam'l	Winchester
Waitstill	Westmoreland
William	Peterborough
Scribner, Screbnenr,	
Benjamin	Salisbury

Scribner - Cont'd

Benjamin, n.	Sandwich
Edward	Salisbury
Edward Jr.	Salisbury
Iddo	Salisbury
John	Salisbury
Nath'l	Sandwich
Sam	Salisbury
Samuel	Wakefield
Scruten, Thomas	Barrington
Searle, Jonathan	Salisbury
William	Salisbury
Searls, Jon'a	Nottingham West
Thos.	Nottingham West

Seavey, Seiva; see also Seavy,
   Seveay, Sevey;

Amos	Rye
Andrew	Nottingham West
George	Deerfield
Ithamar	Rochester
James	Rye
John	Newcastle
John	Portsmouth
Joseph	Rye
Mark	Portsmouth
Moses	Rye
Paul	Rye
Sam'l	Rochester
Sam'l Jr.	Rye
Thomas	Portsmouth
William	Rye
William Jr.	Rye
Seavy, Hennery	Epsom
Joseph	Epsom
Seaward, Georg	Barrington
Giles	Portsmouth
Henry	Portsmouth
John	Portsmouth
Joseph	Portsmouth
Shackford	Portsmouth
Seccomb, Simmons	Kingston
Seecombe, John	Amherst
Seeton, James	Amherst
Seetown, John	Amherst

Seiton, Charles	Lebanon

Selley; see also Selly, Silley;

Moses	Salisbury
Thomas	Seabrook
Selly, Benjamin	Weare
Jacob	Seabrook
John	Hawke
John	Seabrook
Samuel	Weare
Thomas Jr.	Seabrook
Senter, Sam'l	Londonderry
Thomas	Londonderry
Servise, Samuel	Portsmouth
Seve, Elijah	Barrington
Seveay, John	Portsmouth.
Sever, Caleb	Kingston
Robert	Raby
Thomas	Kingston
Thomas Jr.	Kingston
Severance, John	Kingston
Sam'l	Kingston

Sevey; see also Seavey, Seavy,
   Seveay;

Henery	Barrington
John	Chester
Joseph	Rye
Samuel	Rye

Seyner,

Peter Johnson	Rye

Shackford,

John Jr.	Chester
Sam'l	Newington
Samuel Jr.	Newington
Theod'r	Chester
Shannon, Nath'll	Portsmouth
Shapley, Reuben	Portsmouth

Sharborn,

Joseph	Epsom

Sharlay,

Alexander	Wilton
James	Wilton
Samuel	Wilton

Sharman,

Richard	Portsmouth

Shattock, Sires	Hinsdale		Shelden,	
Shattuck, Sheattuck,			Abraham	Temple
Benj., s.	Raby		Samuel	Wilton
Isaac	Raby		Shepard,	
Nat'el	Temple		Daniel	Boscawen
Shaw, Benjamin	Nottingham		James	Canterbury
Benjamin, n.	Sandown		James, n.	Hampstead
Benj. Brown	Hampton		John (Col.) n.	Amherst
Caleb	Kensington		Jno. Jr.	Amherst
Daniel	Lee		John, n.	Gilmanton
Deniel Jr.	Raby		John, n.	Nottingham
David	Kensington		Joseph, n.	Epping
Ebenezer	Rindge		Joshua	Alstead
Edward	Hampton		Oliver	Alstead
Edward	North Hampton		Samuel	Meredith
Elihu	Kensington		Samuel (Dr.) n.	Stratham
Folensby, n.	Sandown		Sheperd, Isaac	Deerfield
Gideon	Hampton		Jacob	Barrington
Ichabod, n.	Monadnock		Jon'th Jr.	Alstead
Ichabod Esq., n.	Sandown		Shepherd,	
Jere'h	Hampton		Jonathan	Alstead
John	Brentwood		Nathaniel	Alstead
John	Nottingham		Roswell	Alstead
John Jr.	Nottingham		Simeon	Alstead
Jonathan	Brentwood		Thos.	South Hampton
Jonathan	Hampton		Sherbon, James	Loudon
Jonathan, n.	Monadnock		Sherborn,	
Joseph	Brnetwood		Samuel	Northwood
Joseph	Kensington		Sherborne, Eph'm	Lee
Joseph	Portsmouth		Samuel	Wakefield
Joshua	Hampton		Sherburn; see also Sharborn,	
Moses	Kensington		Shurburn;	
Moses Jr.	Kensington		Andrew	Portsmouth
Nathan	Kensington		Edw'd	Portsmouth
Richard	Epping		Isaac	Barrington
Samuel	Brentwood		John	Barrington
Samuel	Epping		John	Northwood
Samuel	Hampton		Sherburne, Sheburne,	
Stephen	North Hampton		D.	Portsmouth
Sheafe,			Daniel	Saville
James, n.	Portsmouth		George	Loudon
Jno. Jr.	Portsmouth		Henry	Portsmouth
Jacob Sr.	Portsmouth		Jacob	Loudon
Shed, William	Windham		John	Portsmouth (2)

Sherburne - Cont'd	
John, n.	Portsmouth
Nath'l	Portsmouth
Nathaniel	Portsmouth
Noah	Newcastle
Sam.	Portsmouth
Thomas	Portsmouth
Thomas Jr.	Portsmouth
William	Portsmouth
Sheriar, John	Deering
Sherman, Sheurman,	
David	Richmond
Sherref, Samuel	Portsmouth
Sherwin, Asa	Rindge
John	Rindge
Jonathan	Rindge
Samuel	Rindge
Shillaber, Jon'a	Portsmouth
Joseph	Portsmouth
Shirla, James	Chester
William	Chester
Shirley, Hugh	Chester
Shores, James	Portsmouth
James Jr.	Portsmouth
Peter	Portsmouth
Peter Jr.	Portsmouth
Wm.	Portsmouth
Showers, John	Portsmouth
Shurburn; see also Sharborn,	
Sherburn, Sherburne;	
John	Epping
Richard	Epping
Shurburne, George	Portsmouth
Shute, Jacob	Concord
John	Concord
John, n.	Newmarket
Michael, n.	Newmarket
Walter, n.	Newmarket
Will'm, n.	Newmarket
Sias, Benjamin	Loudon
Charles	Loudon
John	Lee
Joseph	Lee
Sibley, Jacob	Hopkinton

Sibley - Cont'd	
Jonathan	Stratham
Samuel	Meredith
Silley; see also Selley, Selly;	
Samuel	Seabrook
William	Gilmanton
Silsby, Henry	Acworth
Henry Jr.	Acworth
Jonathan	Acworth
Julius	Acworth
Lasell	Acworth
Sam'l	Acworth
Silver,	
Daniel, n.	Salem
Daniel Jr. n.	Salem
Samuel	Hopkinton
Thomos	Salem
Simes, Joseph	Portsmouth
Simond, Ebenezer	Concord
Simonds, John	Rindge
Timothy	Concord (2)
William	Chesterfield
Simons, Eli	Canterbury
Jiosh	Canterbury
John	Weare
William	Alstead
William	Canterbury
Simpson,	
Alex'dr	Windham
And'w	Nottingham
Dalton	Deerfield
John	Deerfield
John	Newcastle
Robt.	Pembroke
Sims, William	Claremont
Simson, Benj.	Canterbury
John	Hampstead
John	Windham
Joseph	Pembroke
William	Windham
Sincklear,	
Richard, n.	Stratham
Sinclear,	
Thomas	Meredith

Sincler; see also Sincklear,		Smart - Cont'd	
Sinclear, Sinklar, Sinkler;		David	Newmarket
Benjamin	Meredith	Josiah, n.	Newmarket
Singleton, John	Kingston	Robart	Candia
Sinklar, Thomes	Sanbornton	Robert	Sanbornton
Sinkler, James	Brentwood	Samuel, n.	Newmarket
John	Stratham	Winthrop	Barnstead
Richard	Barnstead	Smarte, Charles	Newmarket
Richard	Sandwich	Smith,	
Sisco, Elezer	Saville	Abraham	East Kingston
Wm.	Saville	Abraham Jr.	East Kingston
Skinner, Abner	Surry	Alexander Gorden	Brentwood
Amos	Packersfield	Amos	Chesterfield
Slade, John	Alstead	Asael	Salem
John Jr.	Alstead	Benj'n	Bedford
Samuel	Portsmouth	Benjamin	Chesterfield
Slapp, John	Lebanon	Benjamin	East Kingston
John Jr.	Lebanon	Benj.	Epping
Simon P.	Enfield	Benjamin Jr.	Epping
Sleeper,		Biley	Candia
Beainjman	Kingston	Chase	Brentwood
Da'd	Sandown	Christopher	North Hampton
Edmund	Chester	Cornelius	Surry
Edward	Kingston	Daniel	Amherst
[?] Jacob	Gilmanton	Daniel	Kingston
John	Kingston	Daniel	Seabrook
John	Sandown	Daniel	Winchester
John B.	Kingston	David	Exeter
Jonathan, n.	Brentwood	David	Kensington
Jonathan Jr.	Brentwood	David Jr.	Rye
Jonathan	Kingston	David	Stratham
Nehemiah	Hawke	Ebenezer	Meredith
Richard	Kingston	Edward	Gilmanton
Samuel	Sandown	Edward	Newmarket
Trustham	Rye	Edward	Pembroke
William	Kingston	Edward	Sandwich
Sloper, Joshua	Barrington	Elias	Londonderry
Small, Isaac	Lee	Elias	Sandwich
Joseph	Amherst	Eliphalet	Deerfield
William	Amherst	Elisha	Sanbornton
William Jr.	Amherst	Elisha	Winchester
Smart, Benj.	Epping	Ezekiel	Henniker
Caleb	Hopkinton	Francis	Hopkinton
Charles Jr.	Newmarket	Garlen	Barrington

Smith - Cont'd		Smith - Cont'd	
Henry	Rindge	Moses Jr.	Chesterfield
Holab	Richmond	Moses	Henniker
Ichabod	Surry	Nath'l	Conway
Isaac	Amherst	Nathanil	Hinsdale
Isaac	Gilmanton	Nath'l	Londonderry
Isaac	Newcastle	Nicholas	Brentwood
Jabez	Barrington	Nicholas	Candia
Jabez	Brentwood	Obadiah	Candia
Jacob	Amherst	Obadiah	Gilsum
Jacob	Kingston	Page	Nottingham West
Jacob	Sanbornton	Pain	Gilmanton
Jacob	Sandwich	Pearson	Meredith
Jacob	Unity	Reuben	Brentwood
James	Bedford	Richard	East Kingston
James	Hopkinton	Richard	Seabrook
Jedediah	Acworth	Robert	Brentwood
Jess	Salem	Robert, n.	Epping
John	Bedford	Robt.	Londonderry
John	Londonderry	Robert	Peterborough
John	New Boston	Robert	Salisbury
John	Peterborough (2)	Robert	Windham
John	Salem	Ruben, n.	New Boston
John	Seabrook	Samuel	Acworth
Jonathan	Amherst	Sm'll	Allenstown
Jonathan	Candia	Samuel	Epping
Jonathan	Loudon	Samuel	Hopkinton
Jonathan	Meredith	Samuel	Lee
Jonathan	Salem	Samuel	New Boston
Jon'a. Jr.	Sanbornton	Samuel, n.	New Boston
Jonathan	Surry	Samuel	North Hampton
Jonathan Jr.	Surry	Samuel	Nottingham West
Joseph	Brentwood	Samuel	Pembroke
Joseph	Chester	Samuel	Surry
Joseph	Loudon	Samuel	Stratham
Joseph	Newmarket (2)	Samuel (Capt.)	n., Winchester
Joseph	Stratham	Simeon	Sandwich
Joseph	Windham	Solomon	Salem
Jos'h	Chesterfield	Solomon Jr.	Stratham
Joshua	Brentwood	Theophilus	Exeter
Josiah	Deerfield	Thomas, n.	Brentwood
Josiah	Epping	Thomas	Surry
Josiah	Hopkinton	Timothy	Amherst
Moses	Chesterfield	Timothy	Nottingham West

Smith - Cont'd	
Timothy	Sanbornton
Uriah	Wilton
William	Deerfield
William	East Kingston
William	Gilmanton
William	Londonderry
William	Peterborough
William	Salem (2)
William	Society Land
Winthrop	Newmarket
Snell, John, n.	Lee
Reuben	Portsmouth
Samuel	Lee
Thomas	Barnstead
Snow, Amos, n.	Claremont
Daniel	Keene
John	Chesterfield
John	Westmoreland
Joseph	Wilton
Warrin	Chesterfield
Solter, John, n.	Dunbarton
Spafford, David	Temple
Eldad	Temple
Spaford, Moses	Claremont
Spaulding; see also Spoldin;	
William	Raby
Spear, Robert	Windham
William	Peterborough
Spence, Keith	Portsmouth
Spencer,	
Ebenezer	Barrington
Jere'm	Claremont
John	Claremont
Robt.	Keene
Ruben	Claremont
Spinney, John	Packersfield
Spoldin, Stephen	Henniker
Sprague,	
Elkanah	Lebanon
John	Claremont
John	Richmond
Sam'l	Lebanon
Spriggens, William	Newmarket

Spring, Jedidiah	Conway
Sprought,	
Michael	Keene
Stacey, David	Westmoreland
Joseph	Exeter
Standly, Jacob	Amherst
Stanford, Caleb	Dublin
Daniel	Sandown
Phinehas	Dublin
Stanhope,	
Joseph	Packersfield
Stanle, Jonathan	Hopkinton
Stanley; see also Standly,	
Stanle, Stanly;	
Jeduthun	Rindge
Joseph	Rindge
Matthew	Hopkinton
Sam'l	Amherst
Samuel	Hopkinton
Samuel	Rindge
Wm.	Hopkinton
Stanly, Joseph	Hopkinton
Stannard,	
William	Newport
Stanwood,	
Nehemiah	Salem
Will'm	Portsmouth
Starbird, Simeon	Barrington
Stark, Samuel	Derryfield
William, n.	Dunbarton
Starns, Abijah	Chesterfield
Starret, David	Derryfield
Start, Georg	Temple
John	Temple
Stavers, John	Portsmouth
Stearns; see also Starns;	
John	Winchester
Jonas	Chesterfield
Nathaniel	Hinsdale
Stebbens, Josiah	Winchester
Mehuman	Acworth
Steel, Benjamin	Wilton
Clem't	Wakefield
Clem't Jr.	Wakefield

Steel - Cont'd	
David	Peterborough
James	Bedford
James, n.	Claremont
John	Londonderry
Joseph	Amherst
Joseph Jr.	Amherst
Joseph	Londonderry
Thomas	Peterborough
William	Londonderry
Stephens,	
Benjamen	Newmarket
Daniel	Amherst
Elehu	Claremont
Henry	Claremont
Samuel	Barnstead
Sterling, Hugh	Conway
Sterne, T.	Claremont
Steven, John	Concord
Stevens, Steevens, Steivens,	
Aaron	Concord
Bartholomew	Wilton
Benjamin	Deerfield
Benjamin	Kingston
Benjamin	Newmarket
Cotton Mather	Portsmouth
Cutteing	Salisbury
Daniel	Gilmanton
Ebenezer	Brentwood
Ebenezer	Derryfield
Ebenezer	Gilmanton
Eben'r	Kingston
Eben'r Jr.	Kingston
Edward	Brentwood
Elihu Jr.	Claremont
Enoch	Newmarket
Ezekiel	Derryfield
James	Concord
John	Boscawen
Jno.	Concord
John	Kingston
John	Wilton
Jonathan	Dunbarton
Jonathan	Lee

Stevens - Cont'd	
Jonathan	Salem
Joseph	Stratham
Joshua	Nottingham
Joshua, n.	Sandown
Josiah	Claremont
Josiah	Newport
Moses	Hampstead
Nathaniel	Brentwood
Nathanael	Lee
Nathaniel, n.	Stratham
Oliver	Rindge
Parker, n.	Hampstead
Peter Resewell	Boscawen
Phinhas	Concord
Roger	Loudon
Samuel, n.	Brentwood
Samuel	East Kingston
Samuel	Lee
Samuel	Sandown
Simon	Canterbury
Stephen	Lee
Theodore	Wilton
Theophilus	Epping
Theophilus Jr.	Epping
Timothy	Hampstead
William, n.	Brentwood
William, n.	Hampstead
William	Lee
Steward,	
John, n.	New Boston
Sameal	Amherst
Simpson	Amherst
Stewart,	
Alexander	Peterborough
James	Dunbarton
John	Londonderry
John, n.	Londonderry
Thomas	Peterborough
Stickney,	
Amos	Amherst
Anth'y Som'y	Chester
Dan.	Concord
Daniel	Hopkinton

Stickney - Cont'd	
Edmund	Chester
Jonathan	Concord
Lemuel	Pembroke
Thos.	Concord
Stickny,	
Siles Richard	Temple
Stiles, Abner	Wilton
Barnard	Canterbury
Jer	Keene
John	Temple
Joseph	Wilton
Samuel	Barrington
Stinson,	
Archabel	Dunbarton
John, n.	Dunbarton
John	Londonderry
Nathan	Londonderry
Robart	Pembroke
William, n.	Dunbarton
Stockbridg, Israel	Stratham
Stockbridge,	
Abraham	Stratham
Isaac, n.	Stratham
Jacob	Bow
John	Stratham
John Jr.	Stratham
Stocker, Samuel	Hopkinton
Stockwill, David	Croydon
Stoddard, Thomas	Hinsdale
Stoddert,	
David Jr.	Chesterfield
Stokes,	
Benjamin	Nottingham
Stone, Abel	Rindge
Benj.	Atkinson
Benj.	Piermont
David	Chesterfield
Eliph'a	Monadnock
Elisha, s.	Monadnock
Ezekiel	Henniker
James, n.	Henniker
Josiah	Temple
Matthias	Claremont

Stone - Cont'd	
Salmon	Rindge
Silas	Dublin
Silas Jr.	Dublin
Thomas	Henniker
Thomas Jr. n.	Henniker
Uriah	Piermont
Stoodley, Stoodly, Studely,	
Gupey	Portsmouth
James	Newington
James Jr.	Portsmouth
John	Newington
Thomas	Portsmouth
Storrs, Const.	Lebanon
Huckens	Lebanon
Nathaniel	Lebanon
Story, David	Dunbarton
Jeremiah	Hopkinton
Jeremiah Jr.	Hopkinton
Joseph	Hopkinton
Nathan	Hopkinton
William	Lempster
Zechariah	Hopkinton
Storry, Daniel	Dunbarton
Stowel, Enoch	Winchester
Israel	Winchester
Joseph	Winchester
Straw, Strow,	
David	Sandown
Ebenezer	Epping
Ezekiel	Hopkinton
Ezra	Epping
Gideon	Nottingham
Israel	Weare
Jacob	Hopkinton
Joethent	Sandown
John	Epping
John	Sandown
Jonathan, n.	Deering
Jonathan	Hopkinton
Moses	Hopkinton
Richard	Hopkinton
Samuel	Weare
William	Epping

Streater, Joseph	Richmond	Swasey - Cont'd	
Streeter, Amos	Chesterfield	Joseph Jr.	Exeter
Ebenezer	Chesterfield	Sweasy; see also Swasey, Sweazy;	
Enoch	Chesterfield	John Jr.	Meredith
James	Rindge	Sweat; see also Swett;	
Josiah	Chesterfield	Benjamin	Concord
Zebulon	Winchester	Benjamin	Kingston
Strickland, John	Nottingham West	Elisha	Kingston
Strongman,		Enoch	Weare
Henry	Dublin	John Darling	Kingston
Richard	Dublin	Nathan	Kingston
William	Dublin	Samuel	Kingston
Stroud, John	Packersfield	Stephen	Kingston
Strow, see Straw.		Thomas	Loudon
Stuard, David	Kensington	Sweazy; see also Swasey, Sweasy;	
Jonas	Claremont	Benjamin	Exeter
Stuart, Charles	Peterborough	Benjamin	Meredith
Robert	Nottingham West	Sweet, Jonathan	Richmond
Samuel	Dunbarton	Sweetser, Nath'l	Chester
Thomas	Londonderry	Swett; see also Sweat;	
Thomas	Society Land	David	Portsmouth
Studely, see Stoodley.		James	Portsmouth
Stuert, Stephen	Kingston	Jon'a.	Portsmouth
Sullaway, John	Bow	Joseph	Pembroke
Sumner,		Swinerton, Benj.	Croydon
Benjamin (Capt.) n., Claremont		Symonds,	
Stephen	Portsmouth	Joseph	Hillsborough
William (Dr.) n., Claremont		Samuel	Hillsborough
Swain, Abraham	Meredith	Taft,	
Elias	Meredith	Ebenezer	Chesterfield
Ichabod	Sanbornton	Ephram	Richmond
Jacob	Epping	Nathaniel	Richmond
Johnathan, n.	Barrington	Silas	Richmond
Nathan	Epping	Taggart, Teggeat,	
Richard, n.	Barrington	Archibald	Hillsborough
Swan, John	Dublin	James	Hillsborough
John, n.	Keene	James	Londonderry
Joshua	Salem	James	Peterborough
Phinehas	Salem	John	Peterborough
Simon	Canterbury	Thomas	Londonderry
Timothy	Salem	William	Hillsborough
Timothy Jr.	Salem	Taler,	
William	Peterborough	Jonathan	Brentwood
Swasey, Dudley	Loudon	Tally, Aaron	New Boston

Talpey,		Taylor - Cont'd	
Richard Jr.	Portsmouth	Joseph	Epping
Tande, William	Kingston	Joseph	North Hampton
Tandey, Abel	Salisbury	Matthew	Salem
Tandy, Richard	Brentwood	Nathan	Society Land
Tapley; see also Talpey;		Richard	Leavitt's Town
William	Salem	Richard, s.	Wilton
Tappan,		Samuel	Amherst
Christopher	Sandwich	Samuel	Londonderry
Tarbell, Reuben	Westmoreland	Simeon	Loudon
Samuel	Rindge	Thomas	Gilmanton
Tarble, David	Nottingham West	Thomas (Capt.)	Hinsdale
Tarbox,		William	Amherst
Ebeneser	Londonderry	Tayntor,	
Tarlton, Elias	Newcastle	Jedediah	Monadnock
Elias	Portsmouth	Tebbets,	
James Jr.	Portsmouth	David, Q	Rochester
John	Newcastle	Eben'r	Rochester
Richard	Portsmouth	Edward	Rochester
Tash, John	Newmarket	Edmond	Rochester
Thos.	Newmarket	Elijah, Q	Rochester
Tasker, John	Barnstead	Elijah Jr., Q	Rochester
Taylor, Tayler; see also Taler;		Ezekiel, Q	Rochester
Abraham	North Hampton	Henry	Rochester
Adam	Londonderry	John, Q	Rochester
Benjamin (Lieut.) n.	Claremont	Joseph, Q	Rochester
Benjamin	Sandown	Nathaniel	Loudon
Chase	Sanbornton	Robert, Q	Rochester
David	Londonderry	Teggeat, see Taggart.	
Ebenezer	Winchester	Tempelton,	
Edmund	Packersfield	Adam	Windham
Edward	Stratham	Mathew	Chester
Eliphalet	Northwood	Mathew	Society Land
Henry D.	Hampton	Temple,	
Isaiah	Peterborough	Archelaus	Westmoreland
Joel	Wilton	Benjamin	Amherst
John	Hampton	Eben'r	Amherst
John Jr.	Hampton	Elijah	Westmoreland
John	North Hampton	Templeton; see also Tempelton;	
John	Stratham	James	Peterborough
Jon[a]	Amherst	Matthew	Peterborough
Jonathan Jr.	Brentwood	Tenney, Benjamin	Temple
Jonathan	Sanbornton	Tenny, David	Barrington
Joseph (Lieut.)	Claremont	Jonathan (Cornett) n.	Salem

Tenny – Cont'd		Thompson – Cont'd	
William	Monadnock	James	Londonderry
Tewksbury, see Toxbury, Tuxbury		John	Londonderry
Thayer, Allis	Richmond	John	Portsmouth
Ebenezer	Hampton	Jonathan	Lee
Grindul	Richmond	Joseph	Rochester
Jeremiah	Richmond	Moses	Deerfield
Jeremiah Jr.	Richmond	Richard	Rindge
Nehemiah	Richmond	Robert, n.	Lee
Simeon	Richmond	Samuel	Concord
Thing,		Sam'l	Kingston
Bartholomew	Brentwood	Sam'l	Portsmouth
Dudlay	Brentwood	Silas	Chesterfield
Eliphelet	Brentwood	Solomon	Lee
James P.	Portsmouth	Thomas	Kingston
John	Brentwood (2)	Thomas	Portsmouth
Jonathan	Brentwood	William	Portsmouth
Joseph	Exeter	Thomson,	
Josiah	Brentwood	Benjamin	Croydon
Nethll	Brentwood	Benoni	Croydon
Peter	Brentwood	Hugh	Derryfield
Samuel	Brentwood	Ichabod	Rindge
Stephen	Exeter	Jacob	Newmarket
Winthrop	Exeter	Job	Alstead
Thirstin, John	Deerfield	John, n.	Alstead
Thirston, Josiah	Stratham	John	Rindge
Moses	Unity	Joseph	Conway
Stephen, n.	Newmarket	Moses	Sanbornton
Thissel, Josiah	Salem	Robert	Londonderry
Thom, Benj.	Windham	Sam'l	Londonderry
Isaac	Windham	Seth	Weare
Will'm.	Windham	Timothy	Richmond
Thomas, Thomos,		Thorn, Barnet	Hawke
Charles	Sanbornton	Jacob	Kingston
Elisha, n.	Newmarket	James	Kingston
John, n.	Claremont	John	Kingston
Jonathan	Epping	John	Sanbornton
Nathan	Chesterfield	William, n.	Salem
Nathen, n.	Hinsdale	Thornton,	
Nathaniel	Rindge	Matthew	Londonderry
Othniel	Rindge	Thran, Edward	Canterbury
Samuel	Claremont	Thrasher,	
William	Chesterfield	Barnabas	Richmond
Thompson, E.	Portsmouth	Benjamin	Richmond

Thurber,	
Benjamin	Saville
Hezeriah	Richmond
Jonathan	Richmond
Samuel	Saville
Thurstin, James, n.	Nottingham
Thurston, David	Monadnock
Stephen, n.	Stratham
Thusten, Samuel	Gilmanton
Tibets,	
Jeremiah, n.	Barrington
Ticknor, Elisha	Lebanon
Tiffany,	
Benjamin	Keene
Gideon	Keene
Tilden, Charles	Lebanon
Joseph	Lebanon
Joseph Jr.	Lebanon
Tilson, James	Richmond
Tilton,	
Abraham	Epping
Abraham	Stratham
Benjamin	Kensington
David	Deerfield
David	East Kingston
David	Hawke
David	Sandown
Ebenezer	Deerfield
Eben'r	North Hampton
Elijah	Kensington
Jacob	Portsmouth
Jeremiah, n.	Kensington
Jethro B.	Epping
John	Kensington
John	Sandown
Jonathan, n.	Kensington
Joseph	Kensington
Joseph	Loudon
Joseph	Sandown
Josiah	Deerfield
Josiah	East Kingston
Josiah	Epping
Nath'l	Sanbornton
Phineas	Deerfield

Tilton - Cont'd	
Sherburne	Kensington
Shrburne	Sandown
Timothy	Loudon
Timothy	Sandown
William	Loudon
Tinkham, Jer'h	Westmoreland
Tirrell,	
Samuel Jr.	Bedford
Titcomb, James	Leavitt's Town
Tobie, Rich'd	Seabrook
Todd, Andrew	Londonderry (2)
Joshua	Temple
Tolford, Hugh	Chester
John	Chester
William	Chester
Tompson, Topson,	
Samuel	Londonderry
Tomson,	
Matthew	Stratham
William	Sanbornton
Tongue, Stephen	Kingston
Tonshend, see Townshend.	
Toppan; see also Tappan;	
Christo'r	Hampton
John	East Kingston
Topson, see Tompson.	
Torrey, Daniel	Brentwood
William, n.	Portsmouth
Towl, Anthony	Chester
Bracket	Chester
Caleb	Hawke
Francies	Chester
Isaac	Chester
James	Canterbury
John	Epping
John	Hampton
Jonathan	Hampton
Jonathan Jr.	Rye
Joshua Jr.	Hampton
Josiah	Epping
Josiah	Hampton
Levi	Rye
Nathan	Rye

Towl - Cont'd		Townsend,	
Zechariah Jr.	North Hampton	Aaron	Chester
Towle,		David	Temple
Abr'm Perkins	Hampton	Ebenezer	Chester
Amos	Hampton	Thomas	Henniker
Amos Jr.	Hampton	Townshend, Tonshend,	
Elisha	Hampton	John	Rindge
Jacob	Loudon	Toxbury; see also Tuxbery,	
James	Hampton	Tuxbury;	
James	Hawke	Josiah	Hawke
Jeremiah	Hampton	Tozer, John	Monadnock
Jeremy	Hawke	Richard	Monadnock
John Jr.	Epping	Trask, Nath'l	Brentwood
Joseph	Epsom	Treadway, James	Canaan
Joseph Jr.	Hampton	Treadwell,	
Joshua	Hampton	Charles	Portsmouth
Lemul	Hampton	Jacob	Portsmouth
Nathaniel	Hampton	Nath'l	Portsmouth
Philip	Hampton	Nath'l Jr.	Portsmouth
Philip Jr.	Hampton	W. E.	Portsmouth
Samuel	Candia	Tredick, William	Newcastle
Samuel	Hampton	Treep, Richard	Epsom
Simon	Hampton	Treferrin,	
Simeon	Rye	Robinson	Rye
Zach'r	North Hampton	Trefethen,	
Town; see also Towns;		Abraham	Newcastle
Archelaus	Amherst	Abra. Ter [3d]	Newcastle
Gardner	Dublin	William	Portsmouth
Israel	Amherst	Treffren,	
Israel Jr.	Amherst	John Jr.	Newcastle
Jabes	Londonderry	Treften,	
Jacob	Keene	John 3d	Newcastle
Jonathan Jr.	Rindge	Trickey, Trikey,	
Towne, Francis	Rindge	Frances	Nottingham
Jeremiah	Rindge	John	Newington
Jonathan	Rindge	John	Rochester
Nehemiah	Rindge	John Jr.	Rochester
Thomas	Amherst (2)	Jonathan	Newington
Thomas	Wilton	Joshua	Nottingham
Towner,		Thomas	Newington
Benjamin	Claremont	Thos., n.	Rochester
Benj. Jr.	Claremont	Wm	Rochester
Ephraim	Newport	Tripe, Samuel	Portsmouth
Towns, Elijah	Londonderry	Trotter, Alex'r	Westmoreland

True,		Tucker - Cont'd	
Abraham	Deerfield	Moses	Monadnock
Benjamin	Chester	Richard, n.	Portsmouth
David	Amherst	Swallow	Raby
Elijah	Candia	Tuckerman,	
Enoch	Sandwich	John	Portsmouth
Ezra	Deerfield	Jno. Jr.	Portsmouth
Henry	Hampstead	Tuffts, Thomas	Lee
Jacob	Salisbury	Tufts, Henry	Lee
Reuben	Hawke	Henry Jr.	Lee
Thomas	Seabrook	Turner,	
Trumbel, Simon	Concord	Amasa	Rindge
Trumble, John	Concord	Geo.	Portsmouth
Trundy, Thos.	Newcastle	Thomas	Peterborough
William	Newcastle	William	Candia
Trusdel, Rich'd	Portsmouth	Turril,	
Trussel, John	Hopkinton	William, n.	Deerfield
Trussell, James	Sandown	Tutel, Elijah, n.	Barrington
Tuck, John	Amherst	Tuttle, George	Lee
John	Hampton	James Jr.	Barrington
Tucke,		Jotham	Weare
Benjamin	Hampton	Nicheless	Lee
Jesse	Kensington	Oliver	Claremont
John	Brentwood	Samuel	Claremont
Jonathan	Hampton	Stephen	Hinsdale
Jonathan Jr.	Hampton	Thomes	Lee
Samuel	Brentwood	Tuxbery, Timothy	Weare
Samuel	Kensington	Tuxbury; see also Toxbury;	
Tucker, Abijah	Monadnock	Benjamin	Hampstead
Benj.	Kingston	Isaac	Weare
Benj.	Monadnock	Jacob	Weare
Eben	Salisbury	Thomus	South Hampton
Ebenezer	Hawke	Twambley,	
Ebenezer	Sandown	Benj.	Rochester
Ezra (Lieut.) n.	Henniker	Isaac, Q	Rochester
Ezra	Salisbury	Jon'a	Rochester
Henry	Deerfield	Sam'l	Rochester
Jacob	Sandown	Samuel Jr.	Rochester
John	Kingston	Twiss, John	Amherst
John	Sandown	Jon'a	Amherst
Joseph	Hawke	Twitchel,	
Joseph	Portsmouth	Abijah	Dublin
Joseph	Rochester	Ebenezer	Dublin
Lemuel	Concord	Eleazer	Packersfield

Twitchel - Cont'd		Vance - Cont'd	
Eleazer	Packersfield	William	Londonderry
Gershom	Dublin	Varney,	
Gershom Jr.	Dublin	David, Q	Rochester
Jonah	Richmond	Eben'r, Q	Rochester
Nathan	Winchester	Edward, n.	Rochester
Samuel	Dublin	Elijah	Rochester
Stephen	Dublin	Mordecai, Q	Rochester
Twitchell, Jos.	Dublin	Moses, Q	Rochester
Twombly,		Moses Jr., Q	Rochester
Nathanael	Northwood	Varnum, James	Candia
Tyler,		Varrel, John	Portsmouth
Adonijah	Hopkinton	Vaughan, William	Portsmouth
Asa	Rindge	Veasey, Jon[a]	Brentwood
Daniel	Piermont	Thomas	Stratham
David	Piermont	Veazey, Joshua	Deerfield
David Jr.	Piermont	Samuel	Epping
Ebenezer	Piermont	Vennard,	
Jonathan	Piermont	William	Newcastle
Joshua	Pembroke	Verrell, Solomon	Rye
Moses	Pembroke	Very, Francis	Winchester
Moses	Richmond	Samuel	Winchester
Tylor, John	Londonderry	Vesaay, George	Brentwood
Joshua	Rindge	Vezey, John	Westmoreland
William	Londonderry	Thomas Jr.	Stratham
Underhill, Undarhill,		Vincent,	
David	Chester	Anthony	Newington
Hezekiah	Chester	Virgin,	
John	Chester	Ebenezer	Concord
John Jr.	Chester	John	Concord
Jonathan	Chester	Phinehas	Concord
Moses	Chester	William	Concord
Moses Jr.	Chester	Vose, James	Bedford
William	Chester	Sam'l	Bedford
Upham,		Thomas Vickere	Bedford
Phinehas	Amherst	Waddell, James	Chester
Thomas	Packersfield	Wadile, John	Londonderry
Timothy	Deerfield	Wadleigh; see also Wodleigh;	
Upton, Ezekiel	Amherst	Benjamin	Northwood
Urann, John	Boscawen	James	Epping
Uren, George	Epsom	John	Northwood
Uurin, Alex	Portsmouth	Joseph	Brentwood
Vance, James	Londonderry	Joseph Jr.	Brentwood
John	Londonderry	Joseph	Kensington

Wadleigh – Cont'd	
Joseph Jr. n.	Kensington
Simon	Northwood
Wadsworth,	
Sam'l	Henniker
Samuel, n.	Keene
Wait, Jason	Alstead
John	Alstead
Joseph (Lt. Col.)	Claremont
Waite, Nathan	Pembroke
Wakefield,	
Joseph	Deering
Thos., s.	Amherst
Thos. Jr.	Amherst
Wakeham, Caleb	Rochester
Walch, Mathew	Raby
Walden, Waldon,	
Geo.	Portsmouth
Jacob	Conway
John	Portsmouth
Thomas	Portsmouth
William	Portsmouth
Waldo, Beulah	Alstead
Daniel	Alstead
Edward	Alstead
Waldron, Aaron	Barrington
Isaac	Barrington
Wales, Samuel	Barrington
Walker, Andrew	Bedford
Andrew	New Boston
Andrew Jr. n.	New Boston
Daniel	Portsmouth
Ezekiel	Conway
Gideon	Portsmouth
Isaac	Concord
Isaac	Londonderry
James	Bedford
James	Concord
John	Nottingham West
Joseph	Portsmouth
Joseph	Rochester
Joseph Jr.	Rochester
Mark	Portsmouth
Rich'd	Rochester

Walker – Cont'd	
Robert	Bedford
Robert	New Boston
Robert	Rochester
Sam'l	Chesterfield
Samuel	Portsmouth
Samuel	Rindge
Tim⁰	Concord
Tim'o Jr.	Concord
Timothy	Conway
Tobias	Portsmouth
Wm.	Portsmouth
Wallace, Jas.	Acworth
James	Bedford
James	Londonderry (2)
John	Bedford
John Jr.	Bedford
John	Londonderry
Jonathan	Londonderry
Joseph	Amherst
Joseph	Bedford
Robert	Londonderry (2)
Sam'l	Londonderry
Thomas	Londonderry
Thos. Jr.	Londonderry
William	Amherst
Will'm	Londonderry
Wallas, Waymuth	Epsom
Walles, Abraham	Epsom
Wallias, Ebenezer	Epsom
Wallis, Ebenezer	Rye
George	Bedford
George	Epsom
Joseph	Deerfield
Samuel	Rye
Samuel Jr.	Rye
Walter, Joseph	Canaan
Walton,	
Elisha, n.	Chesterfield
Henry	Westmoreland
Jonathan	Seabrook
Larrance	Chesterfield
Samuel	Seabrook
Thomas	Alstead

Walton - Cont'd	
William	Rindge
Walworth,	
Charles	Canaan
Ward, Cotton	Hampton
Daniel	Brentwood
Jonathan	Kensington
Josiah (Capt.) n.	Henniker
Nahum	Portsmouth
Nathaniel	Kensington
Phinies	Henniker
Richard	Amherst
Ruben	Monadnock
Samuel	Newmarket
Thomas	Loudon
Wardner,	
Frederick	Alstead
Jacob	Alstead
Philip	Alstead
Wardwell, Jere'h	Pembroke
Ware, Moses	Surry
Richard	Portsmouth
Ziba	Winchester
Warner; see also Worner;	
Dan'l, n.	Portsmouth
Job	Westmoreland
John	Westmoreland
Jon'a, n.	Portsmouth
Jonathan, n.	Portsmouth
Joshua	Westmoreland
Joshua Jr.	Westmoreland
Marting	Chesterfield
Tobias	Portsmouth
William	Westmoreland
Warran, Daniel	Salisbury
Warren, John	Society Land
Josiah	New Boston
Warrin, David	Croydon
Warson, Thomas	Rye
Washburn,	
Ebenezar	Claremont
Simeon	Keene
Washer, John	Claremont
Stephen	Amherst

Wason, James	Chester
James	Nottingham West
Robert	Candia
Samuel	Nottingham West
Thomas	Chester
Thomas	Nottingham West
Waterhous,	
Samuel	Portsmouth
Waterhouse,	
George	Barrington
John	Barrington
Timothy	Barrington
Waterman, Silas	Lebanon
Waters, Charles	Portsmouth
George	Portsmouth
Hezekiah	Lebanon
Sam'l	Portsmouth
Sam'l Jr. n.	Portsmouth
Watherspoon,	
Robert	Wilton
Watkin, Theod	Winchester
Watson, Andrew	Lee
Benj., n.	Nottingham
Daniel	Hopkinton
Daniel	Rochester
Daniel	Sandown
David	Meredith
Dudley	Exeter
Ebenezer	Kingston
Elesor	Lee
James	Lee
James, n.	Nottingham
John	Newmarket
John, n.	Nottingham
Jonathan	Deerfield
Joseph	Lee
Josiah, n.	Nottingham
Nathan, n.	Nottingham
Nath'l	Rochester
Nath'l Jr.	Rochester
Nicodemus	Weare
Samuel	Lee
Timothy	Portsmouth
Zebediah	Sandown

Watt, Hugh	Londonderry	Webster - Cont'd	
Moses	Londonderry	John	Hampstead
Watts, John	Londonderry	John	Kingston
Nath'l	Alstead	John	Rye
Waymoth, Dennet	Lee	John	Salisbury
William	Lee	John Jr.	Salisbury
Weare,		John	Weare
Jonathan	Seabrook	Jon^a	Atkinson
Jonathan Jr.	Seabrook	Jonathan Lad	East Kingston
Meshech	Portsmouth	Joseph	Atkinson
Nathaniel	Kensington	Joseph	Hampstead
Weatherbee, see Wetherbee.		Joseph	Weare
Weatherspoon; see also Wather-		Joseph Jr. n., Weare	
spoon, Wetherspoon.		Joshua	Rindge
Ale'r	Chester	Levi	Hampstead
Daniel	Chester	Nathan	Chester
Webb, Azariah	Piermont	Nathan Jr.	Chester
Charles	Piermont	Nathan	Salem
Joseph	Piermont	Nath'l	Gilmanton
Webber,		Nath'l Jr.	Gilmanton
Bennedeictk	Monadnock	Samuel	Allenstown (2)
John	Hopkinton	Samuel	Atkinson
Richard	Hopkinton	Samuel	Temple
Thomes	Hopkinton	Samuel	Wilton
Webster,		William	Atkinson
Benjamin	Kingston	William	Salisbury
Caleb	East Kingston	Wedgwood,	
Caleb	Hampstead	James	North Hampton
Daniel	Chester	John	Newmarket
Ebenezer	Salisbury	Jonathan	North Hampton
Eliphalet	East Kingston	Samuel	North Hampton
Enoch	Conway	Weed, David	Unity
Enos, n.	Salem	David Jr.	Unity
Iddo	Deerfield	Elijah	Unity
Isaac (Ens.)	Kingston	Elisha	Gilmanton
Israel	Atkinson	Henry	Sandwich
Isrell	Salisbury	Henry Jr., n.	Sandwich
Jacob	Kingston	Jacob, n.	Sandwich
James	Salem	John	Piermont
Jeremiah	Salisbury	Jonathan	Brentwood
Jesse, n.	Salem	Moses, n.	Sandwich
John	Atkinson	Nath'l, n.	Sandwich
John Jr.	Atkinson	Nathaniel	Weare
John	Chester	Orlando	Gilmanton

Weed - Cont'd	
Samuel	Unity
Weeks,	
Benjamin	Gilmanton
Cole	Sanbornton
John	Newmarket
John	North Hampton
Joseph	Portsmouth
Joshua	Canterbury
Josiah	Exeter
Mathias	Gilmanton
Noah	Gilmanton
Samuel	Canterbury
Samuel	Gilmanton
Stephen, n.	Portsmouth
William	North Hampton
Welch, Bagly	Sandwich
Benjamin	Portsmouth
Caleb	Canaan
John	East Kingston
Joseph	Kingston
Moses	Kingston
Samuel	Bow
Samuel Jr.	Bow
Willim	Boscawen
William	Nottingham
William	Portsmouth
Welles, Thos.	Lebanon
Wellman,	
Jedidiah	Keene
Reuben	Packersfield
Wells, Wels,	
Benjamin	Sandown
Edwad	Sandwich
Ezekiel	Canaan
Jacob	Sandown
John	Nottingham
Joshua	Canaan
Obadiah	Hampstead
Philip	Dunbarton
Samuel	Rye
Sargent	Sandown
Stephen	Loudon
Thos.	Keene

Wells - Cont'd	
Thomos	Sandown
Wendell, John	Portsmouth
Wentworth,	
Eben'r	Rochester
Elihu	Rochester
Ephraim	Rochester
Geo.	Portsmouth
H.	Portsmouth
Isaac	Rochester
James	Rochester
John	Wakefield
Josh.	Portsmouth
Josiah	Rochester
Mark H'g., n.	Portsmouth
Nicholas	Rochester
Reuben	Rochester
Rich'd	Rochester
Stephen, n.	Rochester
West, Edward	Brentwood
James	Hampstead
John	Claremont
Jonathan	Canterbury
Nemiah	Brentwood
Wilks	Chester
Westcott,	
James	Richmond
Weston, Eben'r	Amherst
Isaac	Amherst
Thomas	Amherst
Wetherbee,	
Abraham	Rindge
John	Rindge
Wetherell,	
Eph'm	Westmoreland
Wetherspoon; see also Wather-	
spoon, Weatherspoon;	
David	Chester
James	Chester
Weymouth,	
George, n.	Gilmanton
Wheatley,	
John	Lebanon
Nath'el	Lebanon

Wheeler, Wheelir,	
Abijah	Salem
Abner	Salem
Abraham	Keene
Abraham Jr.	Keene
Benj.	Salem
David	Monadnock
Ephraim	Chesterfield
Hariden	Westmoreland
James	Chesterfield
James Jr.	Chesterfield
Jeremiah	Concord
Jon'a.	Salem
Joseph	Chesterfield
Josiah	Hinsdale
Nathaniel	Croydon
Nehemiah	Epping
Peter	Chesterfield
Peter	Temple
Peter Jr.	Temple
Plomer	Dunbarton
Samson	Salem
Seth	Croydon
Silas	Salem
Solomon	Kingston
Stephen	Dunbarton
Stephen	Salem
William	Dunbarton
Zadok	Keene
Wheelwright,	
John	Portsmouth
Whellock,	
Jonathan	Peterborough
Whidden,	
Ichabod, s.	Lee
Joseph	Portsmouth
Michael	Portsmouth
Samuel	Portsmouth
Whipple,	
—— Esquire	Richmond
Dan	Richmond
Ichabod	Richmond
Israel	Richmond
J.	Portsmouth

Whipple - Cont'd	
Moses	Croydon
Nathaniel	Richmond
Oliver, n.	Portsmouth
Rufus	Richmond
Samuel	Croydon
Thomas	Croydon
Whitaker, Whiteaker, Whiticker,	
Whitker, Whittaker,	
Asa	Weare
Caleb	Weare
James	Portsmouth
John	Rindge
Jonathan	Atkinson
Jonathan	Sandown
Stephen	Atkinson
Thomas	Atkinson
William	Weare
Whitcher; see also Witcher;	
Benj., n.	Nottingham
Isaac	Brentwood
John	Meredith
Nathanel	East Kingston
Richeard	Brentwood
Seargeant	Stratham
Whitcomb,	
Benjamen	Henniker
Jacob	Henniker
Reuben	Henniker
Whitcombe,	
Charles	Henniker
White, Charles	Peterborough
David	Peterborough
Edward	Newcastle
Enoch	Richmond
Henry	Gilsum
Isaac	Pembroke
John	Chesterfield
John, n.	Keene
John	Pembroke
John	Peterborough (2)
John Jr.	Peterborough
John	Portsmouth
Joseph	Westmoreland

White - Cont'd	
Joshua	Newcastle
Moses	Westmoreland
Nathan	Portsmouth
P.	Portsmouth
P.	South Hampton
Rich'd	Portsmouth
Robart, n.	New Boston
Robert	Newcastle
Sam.	Londonderry
Samuel	Londonderry
William	Bedford
William	Chester
William	Conway
William	Peterborough
Wm.	Peterborough
William	Portsmouth (2)
Whitehorn,	
John	Nottingham
Thomas	Nottingham
Whitehouse,	
Solomon	Pembroke
Turner	Rochester
Unpreet	Pembroke
Whitemore; see also Whittemore;	
Benj.	Nottingham West
Joshua	Winchester
Whiting, Samuel	Rindge
Whitman, Daniel	Westmoreland
Noah	Westmoreland
Whitney,	
Alexander	Henniker
Ephraim, n.	Chesterfield
Ephraim (Lieut.) n., Chesterfield	
James	Winchester
Joel	Chesterfield
Joseph	Surry
Richard	Wilton
Solomon	Rindge
Whittaker, see Whitaker.	
Whittemore; see also Whitemore;	
Aaron	Pembroke
Benj.	Pembroke
Elias	Pembroke

Whittier,	
Francis	Hopkinton
Joseph	Nottingham
Wiar, Adam	Londonderry
Wiear, Jno.	Hampstead
Wier, William	Londonderry
Wigen, Jonathen	Newmarket
Wiggan,	
Chase, n.	Hopkinton
Wiggin,	
Andrew, n.	Stratham
Andr. Jr.	Stratham
And'w, Tertius	Stratham
Benj.	Hopkinton
Chas.	Newmarket
Chase	Stratham
David	Newmarket
Henery	Epping
Henry, n.	Newmarket
Isiah	Wakefield
Issachar	Newington
Jacob	Wakefield
John	Lee
Jonathan	Stratham
Joseph	Newmarket
Joseph, n.	Stratham
Joshua, n.	Newmarket
Mark	Stratham
Nathaniel, n.	Stratham
Nathaniel Jr., n.	Stratham
Nathanel 3d	Stratham
Noah	Stratham
Richard	Stratham
Samuel	Stratham
Samuel Jr., n.	Stratham
Simeon	Wakefield
Simon	Stratham
Thomas	Epping
Thomas Jr.	Epping
Tuftin	Stratham
Tuftin Jr.	Stratham
Walter	Stratham
Winthrop	Stratham
Zeb'n.	Portsmouth

Wiggins, Asa	Newmarket
Wight, Joel	Packersfield
John	Dublin
Wilber, Willbur,	
David	Westmoreland
Joseph	Westmoreland
Nathanael	Westmoreland
Philip	Westmoreland
Philip 2nd	Westmoreland
Wilder, Abijah	Keene
Nathanael	Winchester
Thomas	Keene
Wiley, John	Deering
Zebelen	Lee
Wilkens,	
Archelus	Wilton
Bray	Deering
William	Amherst
Wilkins, Wilckins, Wilkines,	
Abijah	Amherst
Jno.	Amherst
Jonathan Jr.	Amherst
Joshua	Amherst
Nehemiah	Hillsborough
Sam'l, s.	Amherst
Timothy	Hillsborough
Willand, George	Rochester
Willard, Willord,	
Amos	Winchester
Benj.	Keene
Elijah, n.	Winchester
Josiah (Maj'r) n.	Keene
Josiah (Col.) n.	Winchester
Prentice, n.	Winchester
Samson, n.	Winchester
Simon, n.	Winchester
Willoughby	Acworth
Willcocks, Jesse	Newport
Willcoks, Phinehas	Newport
Uriah	Newport
Willcox, Ebezer	Gilsum
Obadiah	Gilsum
Obadiah Jr.	Gilsum
Obadiah	Surry

Willcox - Cont'd	
Obadiah Jr.	Surry
Wille,	
Benjamin	Loudon
Ezekiel	Lee (2)
John	Nottingham
Robert	Epping
Samuel	Lee
Thomes	Lee
Willes; see also Welles;	
Abiel	Lebanon
Nathaniel	Epsom
Willey, Allen	Lempster
David	Lempster
Isaac	Barrington
John	Barrington
Jonathan	Nottingham
Lemuel	Barrington
Samuel	Wakefield
Williams,	
Asa	Enfield
John	Lebanon
John	Lee
John	Portsmouth
Joseph	Hawke
Joseph	Henniker
Obadiah	Epsom
Samuel, n.	Barrington
Samuel	Dublin
Simon	Windham
Thomas	Hampstead
Willis; see also Welles, Willes;	
Benjamin	Keene
Jonathan	Westmoreland
Wills, Steven	Lee
Willson, Adam	Chester
Alexander	New Boston
Archelas	Temple
Benjamin	Winchester
Daniel	Keene
David	Deering
David	Keene
Delivrance	Rindge
Hugh	Peterborough

Willson - Cont'd		Windslo,	
James	Chester	Samuel, n.	Deerfield
James	Londonderry (2)	Wing, John	Richmond
James	New Boston	Joseph	Richmond
James, n.	New Boston	Wingate,	
James	Peterborough	Daniel	Rochester
John	Acworth (2)	John	North Hampton
John	Chester	John	Wakefield
John	Conway	Jos'a	Stratham
John, n.	New Boston	Pain (Rev.) n.	Stratham
John	Peterborough	Samuel, n.	Rochester
Joseph	Keene	Sam'l Jr.	Rochester
Robert	Candia	Wm	Rochester
Robert	Londonderry	Winkall,	
Robert, n.	New Boston	Joseph	Portsmouth
Robert	Peterborough	Winkley, Fra's	Barrington
Sam'l	Chester	Sam'l	Barrington
Samuel	Londonderry	Winn, Abiathar	Nottingham West
Sam'l	Peterborough	Caleb	Rindge
Thomas	Londonderry	Joseph	Nottingham West
Thomas	New Boston	Joseph Jr.	Nottingham West
Uriah	Keene	Winslow, Winslo, Winslew; see	
Wilson,		also Windslo;	
Alex'dr	Windham	Benj.	Nottingham
George	Windham	Ephraim	Kingston
Humphry	Brentwood	Jacob	Kingston
James	Windham	John	Kingston
John	Brentwood	Jonathan	Epping
John	Windham	Samuel	Bow
Joseph	Nottingham West	Sam'l	Kingston
Nath'l	Gilmanton	Zebulon	Candia
Richard	Portsmouth	Witcher; see also Whitcher;	
Robt.	Chester	Benjamin	Canterbury
Sam'l	Londonderry	Nathaniel	Canterbury
Sam'l	Windham	Ruben	Canterbury
Thomas	Concord	Witherell, David	Westmoreland
Thomas	Londonderry	Witherspoon, see Watherspoon,	
Thos.	Windham	Weatherspoon, Wetherspoon	
Will'm	Chester	Withington,	
Wm.	Portsmouth	Francis	Henniker
Wilton, Benjamin	East Kingston	Withrell,	
Winchester, David	Westmoreland	John, n.	Rochester
Jonathan	Westmoreland	Witt, Artemas	Westmoreland
Lemuel	Amherst	Wodes, James	Barrington

Wodleigh; see also Wadleigh;
  Joseph 3d   Kensington
Wodly, Thomas Hampstead
Wollais,
  William   Northwood
Wood,
  Abraham   Chesterfield
  George (Doct.) n. Londonderry
  Isaac   Rindge
  James   Rindge
  John Ellin   Salem
  Jonathan   Henniker
  Jonathan   Winchester
  Joseph   Lebanon
  Joseph   Lempster
  Sam'l   Keene
  Silas   Chesterfield
  Timothy   Rindge
Woodard, see Woodward.
Woodberry, Woodbery,
  Benj.   New Boston
  Ebenezer, n. Salem
  Henry   New Boston
  Henry   Salem
  Nat'l.   Salem
  Zech   Salem
Woodbury,
  Benjamin   Salem
  Israel   Salem
  James   Amherst
  John   Brentwood
  John   Salem
  Nathan   Newport
  Peter   Amherst
Woodcock,
  Michael   Chesterfield
Wooderd, see Woodward.
Woodman,
  Benjamin   Canterbury
  Edward   Lee
  John   Rochester
  Joseph   Barrington
  Joseph   Kingston
  Joseph   Sanbornton

Woodman - Cont'd
  Joshua   Kingston
  Joshua   Lee
  Nathaniel   Salem
  Samuel   Kingston
  Samuel   Lee
  Thomas   Hampton
Woods; see also Wodes;
  Richard   Portsmouth
  William   Keene
Woodward, Woodard, Wooderd,
  Abel   Monadnock
  Eliezer   Lebanon
  Ezekiel   Westmoreland
  George   Raby
  Henry   Lebanon
  Moses   Portsmouth
  Robert   Saville
  Solomon   Monadnock
  Stephen   Monadnock
  William, n. Sandown
Woolley, John Richmond
  Nathan   Richmond
  Thomas   Richmond
Wordner, see Wardner.
Work, Samuel Westmoreland
Works, Robart Richmond
Wormall,
  Daniel   Brentwood
  Sam'l   Brentwood
Wormwood,
  William   Rye
Worner,
  Daniel, n. Claremont
  Daniel Jr., n. Claremont
  Levi, n.   Claremont
Worth, John   Gilmanton
  John   Weare
  Timothy   Hawke
Worthen, Enoch Kensington
  Ezekiel   Chester
  Ezekiel   Kensington
  Oliver   Hampstead
  Samuel   Candia

Worthen – Cont'd	
Samuel	Chester
Samuel	Weare
Worthly,	
Jonathan	Weare
Thomas	Weare (2)
Timothy	Weare
Wright; see also Right, Write;	
Aaron	Hinsdale
Abel	Lebanon
Benjamin, n.	Winchester
Isaac	Amherst
James	Keene
Joseph	Salem
Joshua	Amherst
Membrance	Hinsdale
Oliver	Monadnock
Phinehas	Lebanon
Samuel	Winchester
Write, Benjamin	Lebanon
Wyatt, Josiah	Exeter
Samuel	Sandown
Wyllie, James	Bedford
Wyman,	
Daniel	Nottingham West
Isaac	Keene
Jonathan	Deering
Seth	Nottingham West
Timothy	Deering
Timothy Jr.	Deering
Yardley,	
William	Dublin
Yeaten,	
Benjamin	Newcastle
Joseph	Rye
Yeaton,	
Rich'd	Newcastle
Rich'd Jr., soldier, n.,	
	Newcastle
Robart	Portsmouth
William	Portsmouth
Yong, Benjamin	Barrington

York,	
Christopher	Claremont
Eliphalet	Lee
Garsham	Claremont
John	Wakefield
Jonathan	Claremont
Joseph	Claremont
Joseph Jr.	Claremont
Richard	Brentwood
Richard	Wakefield
Richer	Wakefield
Robert	Lee
Thomes	Lee
Young; see also Yong;	
Aaron	Kingston
Aaron Jr.	Kingston
Daniel	Nottingham
David	Hopkinton
Dudley	Gilmanton
Ebenz	Barrington
Elezer	Barrington
Isaac	Barrington
Israel	Salem
James	Deerfield
John	Barrington
John	Newmarket
John	Peterborough
Jonathan	Canterbury
Joseph	Barrington
Joseph	Deerfield
Joseph	Gilmanton
Joseph Jr.	Newmarket
Joshua	Deerfield
Paul	Barrington
Peter	Barrington
Robert, n.	Salem
Solomon	Barrington
Stephen	Barrington
Wintrup	Barrington
Youngs,	
Ichabod	Gilsum
Joseph	Gilsum

A LIST OF THE TOWNS INCLUDED
IN THE FOREGOING RECORD

Acworth
Allenstown
Alstead
Amherst
Atkinson
Barnstead
Barrington
Bedford
Boscawen
Bow
Brentwood
Canaan
Candia
Canterbury
Chester
Chesterfield
Claremont
Concord
Conway and Locations
Croydon
Deerfield
Deering
Derryfield [Manchester]
Dublin
Dunbarton
East Kingston
Enfield
Epping
Epsom
Exeter [fragment]
Gilmanton
Gilsum

Hampstead
Hampton
Hawke [Danville]
Henniker
Hillsborough
Hinsdale
Hopkinton
Keene
Kensington
Kingston
Leavitt's Town [Effingham]
Lebanon
Lee
Lempster
Londonderry
Loudon
Meredith
Monadnock No. 5 [Marlborough]
New Boston
Newcastle
Newington
Newmarket
Newport
North Hampton
Northwood
Nottingham
Nottingham West [Hudson]
Packersfield [Nelson]
Pembroke
Peterborough
Piermont
Portsmouth

Raby [Brookline]
Richmond
Rindge
Rochester
Rye
Salem
Salisbury
Sanbornton
Sandown
Sandwich
Saville [Sunapee]
Seabrook

Society Land [Antrim]
South Hampton
Stratham
Surry
Temple
Unity
Wakefield
Weare
Westmoreland
Wilton
Winchester
Windham